Be Safe Physically and Mentally

with the Crandall System

By Eric Stalloch

Coauthor Clifford C. Crandall Jr.

Be Safe Physically and Mentally with the Crandall System

ISBN-13: 978-0-6151-9322-9

Third Printing: March 2008
Printed By: Lulu.com

Disclaimer:

Although both the program designer and author of this instructional and informational book have taken great care to ensure the authenticity of the information and techniques contained herein, we are not responsible, in whole or in part, for any injury which may occur to the reader or readers by reading and/or following the instructions in this publication. We also do not guarantee that the techniques and illustrations described in this will be safe and effective in a self-defense or training situation. It is understood that there exists a potential for injury when using or demonstrating the techniques herein or otherwise, herein described. It is essential that before following any of the activities, physical or otherwise, herein described, the reader or readers first consult his or her physician for advice on whether practicing or using the techniques described in this publication could cause injury, physical or otherwise. Since the physical activities described herein could be too sophisticated in nature for the reader or readers, it is essential a physician be consulted. In addition, federal, state, or local laws may pro-hibit the use or possession of weapons or tools descried herein. A thorough examination must be made of the federal, state, and local laws before the reader or readers attempts to use these weapons or tools in a self-defense situation or otherwise. Neither the program designer nor the author of this instructional and informational book guarantees the legality or the appro-priateness of the techniques or weapons or tools herein contained.

Dedication

This book is dedicated to Master Jill Crandall (1950-2002) whose passion for life spread to all who knew her. Her love for children and concern for men and women of all ages was evident every day of her life. She was an extraordinary teacher, and I am a better person for the time she shared with me. I hope this book captures a small part of the spirit that she exemplified.

Eric Stalloch

Eric Stalloch

Acknowledgements

I would like to express my sincere appreciation for those people who helped me make this book a reality.

Grandmaster Clifford C. Crandall, Jr.

This book was made possible by the constant guidance and support of my instructor, Grandmaster Clifford C. Crandall, Jr. He did much more than design the Crandall System; he shared his time, experience, and love of the martial arts with me. I will be forever grateful.

Master Allen Hillicoss

I would like to thank Master Allen Hillicoss for the hours he spent working as the Chief Editor of this book. As Grandmaster Crandall's successor, his exceptional martial arts insight and experience was a welcomed asset to the quality of the documentation of the Crandall System in this book.

Mr. Wayne Handy, Sr.

Chief Instructor Wayne Handy is a direct student of Grandmaster Crandall, and for the first nine years of my martial arts training, Mr. Handy was my instructor. He has given me more than these few words can express, but without him, I would not have many of the opportunities I have today. His martial arts skill, clarity of instruction, enthusiasm, and patience inspired me to embrace the traditional martial arts as a way of life.

My Parents: Tim and Marilyn Stalloch

My parents did more than start me in the martial arts. They provided me with a solid foundation, sparked my interest in writing, and have always been there when I needed them. I will always be grateful for the unwavering support and love they have given me. They are also martial arts instructors in their own right.

My Wife: Gisella Stalloch

I would like to thank my wife, Gisella Stalloch, for her constant support, enthusiasm, and patience. She made many sacrifices to allow me the time to complete this book. She is a dedicated martial arts student and a skilled instructor, and she has helped me to achieve more than I ever could alone.

Instructors and Students in Pictures

Finally, I would like to thank the instructors and students of the American Martial Arts Institute who appear in the photographs of this book for their time and assistance. They are:

Chief Instructor Cheryl Freleigh
Dr. Nicholas Chuff
Mr. David Phillips
Mr. Timothy Stalloch
Mrs. Gisella Stalloch
Mr. Joseph Fiore
Mr. Paul Lilley
Miss Nicole Crandall
Christie Catera
Dale Johnson
Stephanie Chard
Jeremy Cellini
Chris Eaton
Jon Lyon
Christian Kozlowski
Amanda Peterson
Matthew Hillman
Sabrina Kowalski
Natalie Kozlowski
Courtney Morton
Aidan Uvanni
Alex Catera
And a special thanks to Officer Gerald Morton.

Photographs by Eric Stalloch and Clifford C. Crandall, Jr.

Photographs for the back cover and for the author and program designer sections by Stephen J. Teuchert.

About the
Program Designer

Grandmaster Clifford C. Crandall, Jr. is recognized internationally for his contributions to the field of martial arts and his safety awareness programs. His educational experience as a permanently certified superintendent of schools, elementary and high school principal, and classroom teacher, combined with his many years as a professional martial artist gave him the unique combination of knowledge and skills to develop the Crandall System, a program designed to increase personal security in daily life. As founder of the American Martial Arts Institute, he is Grandmaster of American Eagle Style, a traditional empty-hand style of martial arts, and he is Headmaster for the world of Takenouchi-Hangan-Ryu-Matsuno-Crandall, a 300-year old iaido style based on the samurai philosophy of life.

Photo By: Stephen J. Teuchert.

Grandmaster Crandall has authored three books and produced seven instructional videos, two of which have now been formatted into DVDs. One of these DVDs is *Children's Self-Defense and Awareness, Volume 1*, a self-contained program of non-aggressive self-defense for educating school children (level one of the Crandall System). He has taught elementary through high school children self-defense with his *Just Get Away* program, presented his *Women's Self-Defense seminars* for rape crisis centers, universities, and other private organizations, instructed *college credit courses* on self-defense, instructed and certified physical education teachers to implement a *K-12 self-defense curriculum* to meet state required safety standards, and designed safety programs for senior citizens.

Grandmaster Crandall produced and hosted the *Martial Arts Today Show* for twelve years, which aired on NBC to over eight million homes in the U.S. and Canada. For over twenty years, he has raised public awareness regarding safety with his *Secure Living* television public service announcements, by serving as the Central New York spokesperson for McDonald's in safety commercials, and with his television show *Safety and Awareness Today* that presented self-defense and safety topics for all ages on ABC, Fox, and MyTV.

In 1994, Grandmaster Crandall coached and led the first American martial arts team to perform in the People's Republic of China, with letters of introduction from the President and Vice President of the United States at that time. He has also led similar delegations promoting good international relations to other countries including Russia, Japan, and Australia. In 2000, he was inducted into the International Hall of Fame for contributions to the martial arts by a Grandmaster. He also holds a Guinness Book World Record for breaking a board while skydiving, a feat performed in conjunction with a child safety awareness campaign. The Crandall System has been taught successfully for many years in private and public schools and community organizations.

These are only a few of his contributions to safety and awareness education during his over 45 years as a martial artist and educator. For more information about Grandmaster Clifford C. Crandall, Jr., visit www.amai-eaglestyle.com.

About the Author

The author, Eric Stalloch, has been a student of the martial arts for over 18 years. His first nine years of training were under one of my top students, Chief Instructor Wayne Handy, whose tutelage and encouragement brought him to a high level of martial arts skills. Over the past seven years Eric has become a student of Do – one's way or path through life – directly under my instruction in regards to philosophy and physical objectives. During this time, his love of the arts has led him to become a senior instructor of American Eagle Style, and his dedication enabled him to become a proprietor of one of the full-time locations of the American Martial Arts Institute.

Photo By: Stephen J. Teuchert.

Throughout his training, Eric has represented our traditional techniques and philosophies in national and international tournaments and seminars. He made exceptional performances in the kata and sparring divisions of the Russian International Tournament in 1997 in St. Petersburg, and he also shared his enthusiasm for the arts when teaching katas in Australia during the American-Australian Martial Arts Exchange in 2005. His demonstration of American Eagle Style has brought him the respect of fellow competitors from around the world and has shone a positive light on American martial artists.

As a result of his belief in the martial arts as a positive, fulfilling way of life, Eric began documenting the seminars of various stylists who performed for our school in articles which have been published in numerous magazines and New York State newspapers. These martial artists have included Master Fumio Demura, Headmaster Tsuneyoshi Matsuno, Master Mark Shuey, Master Frank Dux, and Master Alan Goldberg, to name a few.

10

Eric has also published articles regarding our school's many martial arts exchange trips, including those to Japan and Australia. His journalism skills conveyed his pride and love for the arts, and have brought recognition to very positive aspects of America's martial artists.

Eric also has an extensive educational background, centered on his Permanent New York State Teaching Certification with over seven years experience teaching biology to grades 10-12. I believe this has given Eric the added insight on how to reword or restructure his teaching style to instruct people regardless of their age. This unique skill, coupled with his Master's Degree from Syracuse University in Science, provide him with essential verbal skills and anatomical knowledge to understand and explain a technique down to the very muscle and bone structure of an individual.

Over the past year Eric has impressed me with his work ethic and determination to accurately present "The Crandall System" in this book. His efforts have more than pleased me – they have given me a feeling of pride in him and one of fulfillment that my program is now easily available to everyone. I hope he continues as a student of Do, and that the martial arts remain one of his passions.

--Clifford C. Crandall, Jr.
Grandmaster of American Eagle Style

Introduction

Personal safety is a skill that you use everyday of your life. It involves being aware of vulnerabilities and dangerous situations, taking a proactive approach to prevent dangerous situations from occurring or escalating, applying knowledge of how to capitalize on your surroundings in an emergency, and using self-defense skills for physical action. As with all skills, the skill of personal safety improves when you increase your knowledge about the subject and as you practice the skill regularly. Ultimately, the ability to dance, play sports, drive a car, or perform a self-defense technique is contained within the mind's ability to direct the body. When someone fails to react in a situation, whether they are a child or senior citizen, it is most often because the mind lacks the necessary knowledge on how to respond. In effect, the mind is overwhelmed by the emotions and the confusion of the situation. The mind is like a computer; it can only function as it has been programmed too. The mind is the strongest part of the body and the most powerful self-defense resource you possess. Arming the mind with knowledge and developing the self-confidence to take action can make a significant difference in defending yourself in potentially dangerous situations.

Life is full of situations that can make you feel out of control of the world that surrounds you. The Crandall System's goal is for you to gain the knowledge and the self-confidence that stems from that knowledge necessary to take control and feel safe physically and mentally in your daily life. It is not a martial arts style; it is an organized method for improving self-defense and awareness for all ages. The Crandall System has four levels: Children's Self-Defense and Awareness, Teenager's Self-Defense and Social Awareness, Women's Self-Defense and Assault Prevention, and Senior Citizen's Self-Defense and Secure Living. Each level is intended for a specific audience in order to increase their awareness regarding the dangers that face them in their daily lives and to provide them with effective solutions, but each level also represents a progression of development toward secure living. Therefore, information covered in one level may also pertain to another. Where appropriate, these points of information are identified.

The term secure living was formulated by Grandmaster Clifford C. Crandall Jr., the founder and head of the American Martial Arts Institute and American Eagle Style. Grandmaster Crandall's concern for the safety of others led him to develop several safety programs and to author the *Best Handbook to Secure Living*. In that book he defined the term secure living as "a state of feeling comfortable, at home, in control of the world that surrounds you." His unique experience as a permanently certified superintendent, elementary and high school principal, classroom teacher, and professional martial artist gave him the necessary combination of knowledge and skills to develop the Crandall System. This book represents the growth of Grandmaster Crandall's different safety awareness programs into a documented system for achieving secure living for everyone.

While this book documents the Crandall System, it is also meant to be concise. Therefore, I have included information about the system that best represents its core philosophy, awareness, and physical responses to situations, but the system also includes a wider variety of techniques and knowledge. More of this knowledge is documented in the instructional DVD, *Children's Self-Defense and Awareness, Volume 1 (3rd edition)* and on the website www.amai-eaglestyle.com.

The Crandall System has been taught successfully for many years in private and public schools and community organizations internationally. Its underlying educational principles and philosophy have made it one of the most proactive safety programs in practice today. I am pleased to be able to present the Crandall System. I believe that it will provide you with knowledge that will enhance your mental awareness so that you can be safe both physically and mentally in your daily life.

--Eric Stalloch

Table of Contents

Children
Page 16

Teenagers
Page 40

Women
Page 71

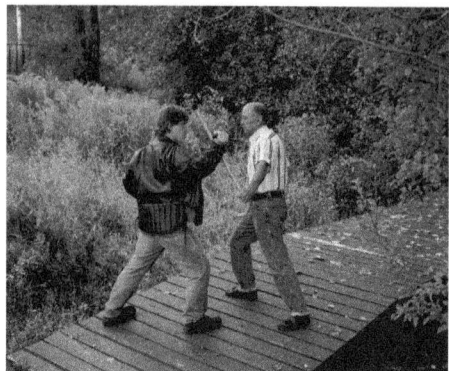

Senior Citizens
Page 116

Level One

Children's Self-Defense & Awareness

Page 16

Presents information for children under 12 regarding safety and abduction prevention. Includes five physical responses to escape assailants.

Level Two

Teenager's Self-Defense & Social Awareness

Page 40

Presents information for young adults between 13 and 19 years old regarding safety and responsible decision making while achieving independence. Includes 16 escape techniques.

Level Three

Women's Self-Defense & Assault Prevention

Page 71

Presents information for women regarding precautions and awareness to prevent physical assault. Includes self-defense techniques with counters.

Level Four

Senior Citizen's Self-Defense & Secure Living

Page 116

Presents information for men and women of all ages but focuses on senior citizens. Topics include safety tips for securing the home and traveling. Covers self-defense with a cane.

LEVEL ONE Children's
Self-Defense & Awareness

Grandmaster Crandall formulated this level based on two parts of his professional life.

>**First**: He was an elementary school principal for kindergarten through fourth grade.

>**Second**: For over 40 years, he has presented a program to preschool and primary school children called Tot-Awareness, which aims to prevent child abduction.

Section One:
Educational Philosophy

This section provides educators and parents with the objectives and teaching philosophy of the Crandall System. The Crandall System educates men, women, and children of all ages regarding dangers that face them everyday and provides them with effective solutions so they may feel more secure in their daily lives. The objectives for mental awareness and physical skills can be achieved by following the four key principles of the Crandall System's educational philosophy.

Objectives for Mental Awareness

1. Participants will understand ways to promote positive behavior from those around them and ways to discourage unwanted behavior.
2. Participants will demonstrate and present personally and socially responsible behavior.
3. Participants will care for and respect themselves and others.
4. Participants will recognize threats to themselves and their friends and will have the confidence to offer safe alternatives to minimize those threats.
5. Participants will understand self-defense, when to use it, and its relationship to others whether they are potentially threatening or simply daily participants in their social surroundings.

Objectives for Physical Skills

1. Participants will perform skills that are basic to small and large motor coordination. These skills will allow them to successfully manipulate and escape physical aggression.
2. Participants will gain the self-confidence to challenge, enjoy, and express themselves positively through their training in self-defense.
3. Participants will be able to identify safety hazards and react effectively to ensure a safe and positive experience for themselves and those around them.
4. Participants will demonstrate care, consideration, and respect for themselves and their partner while practicing the activities.

The educational philosophy of the Crandall System prioritizes awareness, responsible behavior, prevention, and verbalization before any physical action. However, it also recognizes that a physical response is sometimes required. As a parent, educator, or community member, it is important to understand that self-confidence is what makes the difference when taking a stand in a situation that could end up being very serious.

Teaching Self-Confidence and Self-Defense

Self-confidence is a key element in successful self-defense, but teaching it can be challenging. Every student is different. Teaching the physical techniques of the Crandall System involves accepting the following concepts and knowing how to put them into practice for all students.

1. You do not have to touch a child to teach a child

Physical contact by adults is unnecessary to teach a child. Yes, physical contact has short-term benefits for such things as correcting body posture and techniques, but other methods of instruction are more appropriate and effective in the long term. There are several reasons why you should not touch children. This concept is primarily for people working with children who are not their own.

Every time a child is touched, that child is desensitized.

Every time a child is touched, that child is desensitized. The best self-defense is awareness, and a student who is touched often by an adult will begin to feel that this is normal. The child subconsciously learns to accept a level of physical contact that diminishes their ability to react in dangerous situations.

An important step in building self-confidence is establishing trust. Initially, a child derives self-confidence from their parents or instructor.

Teach without touching.

The child must first trust their instructor to establish that self-confidence. Trust has many facets, and two of these are predictable boundaries and consistency. When you touch a child, you implant in their subconscious mind the awareness that they can be touched at anytime. This directly undermines trust and self-confidence

There are many other reasons why physical contact is wholly unnecessary when teaching, including legal considerations, but this book is not meant to be an exhaustive textbook. Therefore, use teaching methods that do not involve physical contact such as demonstrations, verbal directions, imagery, and visual aids. Endeavor to arm the child's mind with knowledge so they will possess the ability to react.

2. Continually use supportive compliments

Encouragement builds self-confidence. Point out what the child does well, not what they could be doing better. It is essential to continually use supportive compliments, smiles, and other forms of positive reinforcement.

3. Be patient

Always be patient, especially when teaching children. A child's body is still developing, and this causes changes in motor coordination, balance, and confidence. These challenges can be frustrating to a child. Through repetition, constructive correction, and supportive compliments, the child will continue to build self-confidence and proficiency with the techniques. Learning is a process that requires time.

4. The key to success is your own enthusiastic attitude

Be aware that a child responds to the atmosphere that you create. If the child is having fun along with you, they will learn faster and will wish to learn more. When you compliment them, use the inflection of your voice to reinforce your own excitement.

Section Two:
Information for Adults

Sometimes we take for granted that children possess the ability to make good decisions regarding their own safety. As you read the following section, you may find yourself thinking that this information is just common sense. Each individual child needs to be taught this information, and they must be reminded of it often before it becomes common sense to them. Please read and pass on this information. Through your efforts, children can learn common sense and become more aware of the world that surrounds them.

Ten Tips for Tots:

Here are ten suggestions that will make a big difference in a child's awareness and responses.

1. **Know your home phone number.** A home phone number is often easier for a child to learn than their address, and it can be more helpful if police find them lost in another city.

2. **Know the color, make, and number of doors of the family car.** An easy way to teach children to recognize the family vehicle is to have them draw and color a picture of it.

3. **Know how to find help.** Children should know that police officers, firefighters, and mail personnel are people they can turn to for help. These individuals are also easy to identify.

4. **Learn directions to your home.** A child within four blocks of home should know how to find it. You can practice this by taking walks with the child.

5. **Never go near a stranger's car.** A child should speak louder if the stranger can't hear or go get a parent to help them, but no one should ever approach the car.

6. **Never let a stranger in your home.** Children who are home alone often are at greater risk and should never open the door. They should direct the stranger to a neighbor and then call you to keep you informed.

7. **Never take ANYTHING from a stranger.** We teach our children not to take treats from a stranger, but a child could just as easily be lured away by something else, such as free movie tickets or toys.

8. **Get an adult to help an adult.** Teach children to get a parent to help another adult.

9. **Don't stay with a group of friends who aren't following the rules about strangers.** If peers aren't being careful, the child should warn them, then leave and tell their parents about what happened.

10. **Know how to break free if grabbed by a stranger.** Teach the child a circular arm breakaway. A potential abductor views a child who takes action as too much effort and will go look for an easier target. This technique is taught on page 35.

Information About Teaching the Ten Tips for Tots

Tip 2: Knowing Your Family Car

It is surprising how many children cannot accurately describe their family's car. Sometimes we overlook the fact that a three to five year old spends a greater amount of their time on the inside of the car looking out. The size of parking lots associated with malls and shopping centers makes this knowledge crucial for the safety of small children. If a young child is separated from their family, they could feasibly be within sight of your car and never notice. Two additional assets for your child's awareness include always identifying a per-

Drawing the family car is a good way to learn how to recognize it later.

manent landmark near the area you have parked and having a specific picture, color sticker, or other item in the window for them to see.

Tip 3: Finding a Helper

As adults, sometimes we assume that children know what to do when lost. Finding help when they are lost is one of the most complicated challenges for a small boy or girl. Children should look for police officers, mail personnel, or fire officials. Their uniforms and vehicles make them easy to identify. Very few people take the time to visit the police station, post office, or fire station to introduce their sons or daughters to a staff member who is in uniform. Yet, this is one of the best preventative practices for their children's safety. Visiting these places will give the child the visual cues needed to remember who to turn to for help. Combined with encouragement from you to turn to these people, it will give your child the confidence they need to seek help. In addition, many malls and shopping centers have security personnel. If you are a regular patron of a particular shopping center, giving a small child an opportunity to meet a security officer in uniform can make a big difference if they become lost. A child may not remember the individual in the uniform, but they will retain the image of the uniform. This will help them identify another security officer in the future.

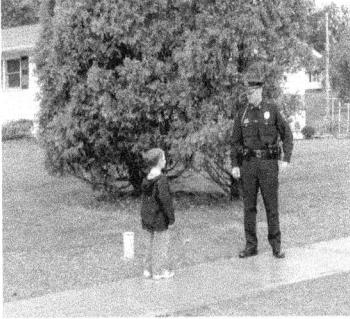

Introduce your son or daughter to a police officer in uniform.

Tip 6: Never Let Strangers in the House

Many children arrive home from school before either of their parents arrives home from work. Unfortunately, a thief or child molester can figure this pattern out in only a few days. This danger presents less of a challenge for teenagers, but younger children are more vulnerable to a stranger's request to use the phone because of an emergency. Children need to be reminded that the door should remain locked to all strangers. It is also important to clarify the wide range of people that make up the group we call strangers. Once we convince children that police officers are helpers that afford benefits and safety, and that it's important to help people who are in real need, we exclude these people from being considered strangers. Even if the stranger indicates that they are a police officer, they should be denied entrance. A child will actually say, "It wasn't a stranger; it was a man who needed help and had to use our phone!" They will say, "It wasn't a stranger; it was a person who said they were a police officer!" When the child is home alone, he or she should be instructed not to let anyone in. It is better for them to direct the stranger to a neighbor's house. These children should have a phone number that they can call immediately. They should also have a place that they can go to for safety if they become afraid and need to leave the house. This might be a neighbor's house, public store, or relative. Discussing the complexities of strangers, helping others, and safety should be done often to meet each child's changing maturity, self-confidence, and understanding of the world that surrounds them.

Tips 7 and 8: Accepting Presents and Helping Strangers

A common ploy by child abductors is to exploit a child's natural desire to be helpful by encouraging the child to help find a lost kitten or puppy. This is an old ploy, but there are still many documented cases of a stranger offering a child a stuffed animal, candy, or toys to lure them closer to a car. It is difficult to determine what goes through the mind of a person who is willing to kidnap and molest a child. It is important to realize that these people exist, and without constant reinforcement, our children will fall prey to them. Our primary defense is educating children that to help an adult, they must find another adult that they already know. You can avoid creating paranoia in your child and still arm them with the knowledge to say, "no,"

To help a big person, find another big person.

by telling them short stories or parables. When you identify in two or three different ways how they can help, you ensure they keep their distance from strangers and their cars. Remind them of the rule, "to help a big person, find another big person."

Tip 8: Freeing Yourself from a Stranger

The circular arm breakaway is presented in section four on page 35. It is also presented for women's self-defense at level three of the Crandall System. An attacker does not grab a child with all of their strength, and they do not expect the child to react. The element of surprise and the physics of the body's anatomy make this technique effective for all ages. The technique uses the strength of the attacker to assist in getting free. The added strength and belief that they can do this will depend on how often you practice and the positive reinforcement and praise you give them.

Labeling Clothing

Many mothers label their small child's clothes for easy identification by writing his or her name on them. Although the labeling is beneficial because it helps little Johnny find his coat when it is piled with fifteen other coats at the preschool center, some things should be considered.

When the child is wearing the coat or clothing, the name should not be visible to strangers. If visible, it becomes easy for a stranger to walk up, say, "Hi, Johnny!" and appear he is a friend who already knows him. Johnny will not realize that his name was read off his sleeve or collar. I have had adults at conferences ask me, "How did you know my name?" They felt a little foolish after I pointed out that it was on their nametag on the front of their shirt. Children will never stop to realize this. If you label a child's clothes, it is better not to use their whole first or last name. An alternative to their name is a color, number, or shape such as a triangle in black magic marker that your son or daughter will look for when gathering up their clothes.

Have a Code Word

Sometimes there are situations when a parent is unable to pick up a child such as a car breakdown or a family emergency, and it becomes necessary for someone else to give the child a ride home. In these circumstances, the child could be put into an awkward situation because they have been taught not to interact or accept rides with strangers. If a neighbor, friend of the family, or relative is able to give them a ride, they should have a way of knowing that you have given them permission to accept the ride. Here it helps to have a word that only the parents and child knows. The word should not be obvious or easily guessed, and the child should know not to tell it to anyone, even friends. In an emergency situation, the parent can tell the person who will pick the child up the word. Once used, the word would need to be changed.

Safe Treats at Halloween

Halloween activities once created familiarity with neighbors, but over the years, safely trick-or-treating on Halloween has become more challenging. Every year we all work to maintain the excitement and fun that we, our parents, and our grandparents remember. Despite these efforts, when children trick-or-treat by themselves in neighborhoods in which they are not familiar, they may be exposed to many actual scary situations. While most people who participate in Halloween are decent, it is important to remember that there are people who intentionally attempt to harm children. The number of possible dangers that can be found in fruit, homemade products, and wrapped candy is too repulsive even to mention. You do need to check the treats your children receive. If possible, find a fun way to share time with your children as you go through the candy and fruit they obtained through trick-or-treating.

When trying to promote the fun and excitement of Halloween, it is important not to become offended by the reluctance of children to accept homemade cookies or candy apples. The child's refusal is not due to disrespect, but one of caution learned from their parents. Through awareness, we can keep Halloween a fun experience for our children and future generations.

The Best Way May Be the Long Way

Young boys and girls should be reminded to avoid shortcuts to and from school or playgrounds. During the few minutes saved, they are unaccounted for and out of sight. To a child, taking a shortcut through a wooded area or behind some houses seems harmless and innocent. Unfortunately, it gives an abductor or child molester their best chance to get at the child without someone seeing them, and it is very difficult to retrace the actions of the child if they turn up missing.

If Someone Bothers Your Child

If a child is bothered while at the playground or anywhere else, they should tell their parents that it happened. You need to remind your children of this, but there is another point to consider, one that can be difficult.

As parents, you should not panic or overreact in front of the child. You shouldn't scold or yell at the child for being somewhere alone. Definitely, you shouldn't forbid them from ever going there again because of what you have just learned. All of these actions punish the child for their willingness to inform you of what occurred. If you punish them out of concern for their safety, it will ensure that they keep the next incident in their lives a secret. It is hard, but you should remain calm, talk with your son or daughter, and let them know how proud they made you. Remind them to stay alert and be careful.

Once you have taken care of your child, you need to take some additional actions. Call the police. Notify the authorities at school and the area where they were playing. You may want to drive down to the playground or school area a couple of times and watch from a distance yourself while your child is there. Your concern is great, but it should not override the positive action your child has taken and the praise they deserve.

Teaching Punches

<u>Proper Fist</u>

Making a proper fist may seem obvious. In fact, there are two or three acceptable ways for a trained martial artist or boxer, but one is promoted the most for individuals who do not train with their fists regularly. It is important to use proper structure for techniques such as the fist, because proper form also protects the parts of the body you are using to defend yourself.

First: Begin with your hand open and palm up with the fingers flat and the thumb to the side. Fold (or curl) your fingers down onto themselves and into the palm of your hand.

Second: Now that the fingers are closed and tight, place your thumb over the first two fingers.

Note: Never fold your fingers over your thumb with it in the center of your fist. If you strike with your hand in this structure, you risk breaking or dislocating your thumb upon impact.

The hand is now closed into a proper fist. Strike with the first two knuckles of your hand when you punch. The fingers with these knuckles are reinforced by the thumb, and striking with the first two knuckles both protects the joints of your hand and maximizes the effectiveness of the strike.

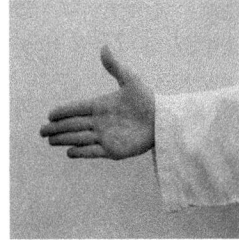

1) An open hand.

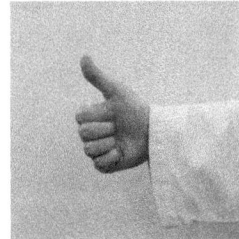

2) Fingers curled down.

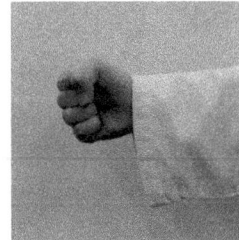

3) Thumb over the first two fingers.

Front View

Horse Stance

A horse stance is a formal way of standing when practicing punches or other techniques. A horse stance has many benefits. It strengthens the quadriceps muscles and provides a sense of balance when learning punches. More importantly, it neutralizes the motion of the body from just above the hips down to the floor. This allows a student to focus on the upper body technique of punching.

Stand with the feet side-by-side and about twice the shoulder width apart. Bend the knees and keep both feet facing forward. The weight distribution should be about 50% on each leg. The shoulders should be directly above the hips. The back should be straight. The eyes should look straight forward and not down.

Horse Stance

Punches

Punch 1

Punch 2

Stand in a horse stance with one arm fully extended in front of your body. The hand should be a proper fist with the palm side down. The other hand should be a proper fist, palm up, in the chamber. When in the chamber, the fist floats near the hip with the elbow straight behind the fist.

To punch, the extended arm and the chambered arm switch places. As the chambered fist punches, it passes the returning fist at the half-way point, and both arms rotate. When the extended arm has completed one punch, its fist is palm-down, and the other fist is palm-up in the chamber. The first two knuckles should lead the punch, and the fist should be directly in front of the elbow during the entire technique. The punching arm should slide gently across the body throughout the entire technique. For a visual demonstration of a proper punch and how to teach punching, please see the Crandall System Level 1 DVD: Children's Self-Defense and Awareness, Volume 1 (3rd edition). See page 155.

How to be a Partner

When practicing punches, have the child use a pillow, punching shield, or couch cushion. Do not let them hit you no matter how strong you feel or how soft their punch. If they can hit you without hurting you, they will not have self-confidence that the technique will actually work.

Use a shield or cushion.

Section Three:
Awareness for Children

This section is written for children to read. Depending on their age, you may want to read these segments with your child, or to your child. You should discuss each of these segments with your children. It will allow you to present the information in a format that best meets their level of intelligence and perceptiveness, and you can answer any questions they may have.

The Buddy System

When you go out to play on the weekends, after school, or during vacation, you should have another friend with you. This is sometimes called the buddy system. The term may seem a little childish, but it is easy to remember. What if you fall off your bicycle, twist your ankle while running, cut yourself on a nail or a piece of glass, or even have an allergic reaction to a bee sting? If you have an accident, your buddy will be able to go for help. Friends look out for one another. What if your buddy gets hurt or needs help? You'll be able to go get help for them. Accidents can

Always have a buddy.

happen. In all of these events and more, having a buddy there who can go get help will make a big difference.

The buddy system plays an important role when you go swimming, too. Sometimes when we go down by a river, creek, lake, or small pond on a hot day, the water looks so nice and cool that we think about going in to swim.

However, going into the water or swimming without anyone else around is dangerous. Accidents can even happen in an area you have been in before. The surface of the water can be very calm and appear smooth or flat, but beneath the surface, the water may be moving or it may be much deeper than it looks. It could also hide sharp or slippery rocks. Swimming in waves and moving water can be fun, but it can also be dangerous without a friend nearby. Most of the time, your mom or dad is your buddy and watches out for you, but if they're not there, you need another buddy with you before you swim. It makes sense to be cautious. If you go swimming, have a buddy with you.

Where are You?

Always tell your parents where you will be going or playing even if it's just next door at a friend's house. There are many good reasons for this. What if you fall or get hurt? As it gets late, your mom or dad will not be able to know where to look for you. What if something special happened? Imagine that your favorite aunt or uncle stops by your home, or a close friend of yours, who had moved away, called to talk to you. I'm sure you would like your parents to be able to find you right away, and they can, if they know where you are.

If You Are Lost (Ages 3-6)

Boys and girls, who can help you if you are lost or separated from your family or friends? There are three good groups of men and women that I call helpers. They wear uniforms and drive special cars that make it easier for you to find them. These people are normally very familiar with the area where you are lost. These helpers are police officers, fire officials, and mail personnel. These people are friendly and know how to find your family. If you are lost, stay calm and find one of the helpers.

Look for a helper's uniform.

Holiday Safety in Stores

During the Thanksgiving and Christmas seasons, the stores become very busy. With so many people out shopping and so much to see and do, you may become separated from your mom, dad, sister, or brother. If this happens and you find yourself all alone, look for the person who runs the cash register. The person at the cash register can help and usually has a microphone that allows them to call for your parents.

Find a cash register.

Who are Strangers?

In movies and television, strangers are usually scary men with dark sunglasses. It is important for you to know who real strangers are. Strangers are anyone that your parents have not told you it's okay to talk with. Even helpers like police officers are strangers. If you need help, you should look for one of the helpers, but if they come up to you, you should go see your mom or dad right away. If you walk home from school and a friendly man, woman, or teenager says, "hello," to you everyday, they are still a stranger until your mom or dad says it's okay to talk to them. At school or the playground, it is good to make friends with other boys and girls, but until your parents meet their parents, you should not go to their house. If you wonder whether someone is a stranger, ask your parents and they will help you.

Rides with Strangers

When school is in full swing, it is a good time to remember that it is not safe to take rides with strangers. Older brothers and sisters, you should remind your younger brothers and sisters not to do this. Sometimes when you walk home from school, it begins to rain or snow. It seems easier to take a ride from a helpful stranger than to walk the rest of the way. Sometime you may miss your bus or ride and be left behind, waiting and wondering what to do. At any time, if someone drives up and offers you a ride home, say "NO." You don't know the person or people in the car.

No matter what they say, don't get in. Say, "no," even if they say your mother sent them to pick you up. Say, "no," even if they say they are your visiting aunt or uncle and that you were a baby when they last saw you. Go back into the school, ask to use the office phone or ask for help, but don't take rides with a stranger, a person you don't recognize. Remember to tell your parents about what happened. They will be proud and help you.

Helping Adults (Ages 3-9)

If a big person driving asks you for directions, or needs help finding something they have lost, like a kitten or puppy, remember this very good rule: To help a big person (an adult) you should go get a big person.

To help a big person, you should go get another big person.

We all want to help other people, but it's important to know how. As you grow up and get older you will be able to help in different ways. Right now, the best way to help is to follow the rule. Tell them to wait, and then quickly get a big person, an adult like Mom or Dad, to help them. Remember, you can help big people by getting another big person.

Never Let Strangers in the House

Many young ladies and gentlemen arrive home from school before either of their parents. While you are alone, don't let strangers into the house. Even if the stranger indicates that they are a police officer, keep the door locked. Police officers are helpers, but unless you ask for their help, they are still strangers. If someone comes to your house and needs help, tell them to go to the neighbor's house. If your parents are home, get your parents. Your parents will give you a phone number that you can call after a stranger comes to your door.

Should You Be Touched?

Boys and girls, there are times when you are touched by someone else while playing, and it is good to know what is okay and what is not. Something that can help is to think of your swimsuit. You see, no one should touch you in the areas where your swimsuit normally covers you. If someone other than your doctor does touch you where your swimsuit covers, you should tell your mom or dad right away. Your parents won't yell at you. They will listen and talk to you about it. Remember, if someone touches you and it doesn't feel right or you are touched where your swimsuit covers, make sure you tell your mom or dad right away.

Crossing the Road

You probably know to stop, look, and listen before you cross the street. Everyone should be careful near the road. You should always check for traffic. Be careful around tall bushes. If you live in an area of our country where snow creates banks, be aware that drivers may not see you. It is difficult to drive a car or truck over icy and slushy roads. High snow banks and blowing or drifting snow make it even harder for drivers to see you. Stepping out between snow banks without looking or sledding and sliding down banks into the road puts your life in jeopardy. Don't walk in the road, even if the sidewalks aren't plowed. As always, take a moment to look both ways before crossing the road, especially during the snowy months in some parts of our country.

Matches Are Not Toys

Matches don't look like they would hurt anyone, but they can hurt you and many other people. You may know that a lit match or lighter can start a fire. Even a small flame from a match or a lighter can burn you, and it can cause an even bigger fire. Even after the flame is out, a match is still very hot and can burn and start a fire. Fires can destroy forests and kill animals. They can also burn down homes and hurt or kill people.

The most dangerous time of the year for a fire is in the summer because the grass is dry and can catch fire easily. I have seen both men and women throw a match or cigarette out of their car window. This can start fires.

Be careful and aware around matches and other items that can cause fires. You young ladies and gentlemen can help by reminding others. Fire is something to be respected, and matches and lighters are not toys.

Caution around Fires

Everyone reading this understands the danger of matches, but it is important to be very careful around all kinds of fire. This is most important during winter and especially the holiday season. Playing around a kerosene heater, wood stove, fireplace, or a lit candle is just as dangerous as playing with matches.

In the colder months, many things are used to help heat the house or create a festive look, and they all need to be respected because they can all cause a fire in your home. A spark can land on clothes, wrapping paper, or even the rug. Once a spark or flame starts, it is very hard to stop.

During the holiday season, the house is filled with decorations and other things that can get in the way of playing. We must be careful not to move them near a fire, or to move a fire near them.

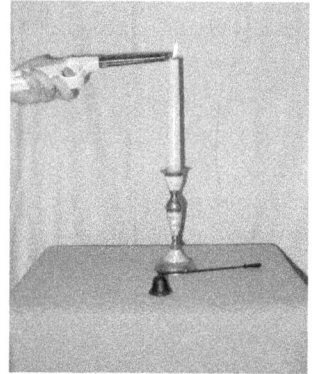

More than matches can cause fires.

We all know about matches, but a fire can start in many ways. The risk of a home tragedy through fire is greater during the Thanksgiving and Christmas seasons. Take the time for a special reminder about this danger. You can help by reminding others.

Guns and Knives are Not Toys

Guns and knives should be treated like matches and fire. They are tools that should be respected. Guns and knives are not toys, and you should not be playing with them as if they were. When we practice self-defense in the martial arts, we use pretend guns and knives because we don't want anyone hurt by accident. Even if you are good at self-defense, there is a good chance of being cut by a knife during an attack.

Unlike a toy knife, a real knife is normally heavier. A real knife can cut you or a friend very easily, causing a lot of pain and stitches, leaving permanent scars. Knives are tools. They can be used for cutting food, carving wood, or cleaning fish. As you get older, your mother, father, or maybe even your grandparents can teach you how to carefully use a knife as a tool to help you, not hurt you.

Guns and Knives

Hunting and fishing are very popular in many parts of the country. If your parents, relatives, or friend's parents have guns, remember that they are not toys. You should not be touching them or looking at them without a parent around. Like knives, your parents might teach you about guns as you get older. If a friend wants to show you a gun, you should remind them that they are not toys, and tell your parents about it. Your parents won't yell at you for being around a gun, and they will talk with you and answer all of your questions.

Remember, friends look out for each other's safety. Guns and knives are not toys, and you or a friend can be hurt or killed very easily by playing with them.

Say "No" to Drugs

No matter what your age, saying "no" to drugs is a constant challenge. It must be met with the confidence that saying "no" is the right thing to do. I realize this is said quite often, but marijuana, pills, powders, household products, and other drugs all take away your freedom of choice. I have had many opportunities to explain to groups of young ladies and gentlemen how dangerous and foolish it is to use drugs

If you use drugs, your life is not yours. It's a dream on the road to becoming a nightmare. There are a great many things you can do with your life. Would you like to be the best football player or the best martial artist? How about becoming an excellent swimmer or cheerleader? You could be a computer expert or someone who reads a lot and shares your knowledge with others. By saying "NO" to drugs, you keep what is yours—the clarity to make good choices. Achieve your goals and dreams. Use your mind and body for a secure and happy life. Don't give them away to drugs.

If you use drugs, your life is not yours.

Section Four:
Escape Techniques

The following physical skills are non-aggressive escape techniques that cannot be used to bully others. They are effective ways for children to free themselves from a potential abductor and seek help. It is hoped that through the awareness gained at this level, the situations where these techniques are needed will never occur.

Circular Arm Breakaway

An attacker typically grabs a child with a straight across wrist grab, a cross wrist grab, or a sleeve grab with the intention of pulling the child out of sight and into a secluded area.

A straight-across wrist grab occurs when an attacker uses his hand to grab the child's opposite arm, like a mirror image. For example, the attacker's left arm grabs the child's right arm.

Straight Across Wrist Grab

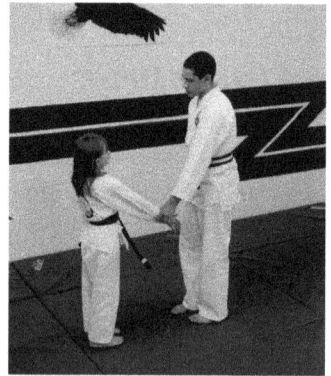

A cross-wrist grab occurs when an attacker uses his hand to grab the child's same arm by reaching across the front of his body. For example, the attacker's right arm grabs the child's right arm.

Cross Wrist Grab

A sleeve grab occurs when an attacker grabs the child's shirt or coat on the upper arm. For example, the attacker's left arm grabs the child's right sleeve.

Sleeve Grab

In all three of these attacks the child can escape using a technique called a circular arm breakaway.

1) The Wrist Grab

2) One Direction

3) The Opposite Direction

4) Once Free, Back Up and Run

The circular motion of this technique involves a change of direction that uses the strength of the attacker to assist the child in escaping from the grab. Swing your arm in one direction, and then quickly reverse direction and complete three or more large circles in the opposite direction. Your arm should be straight, and the large sweeping motion of the circles should come from movement (rotation) at the shoulder joint. The direction of the circles does not matter. Whether you swing clockwise or counter clockwise, both motions are effective to escape the grab. The extra circles you complete once freed are important. They visually distract the attacker and prevent him from immediately grabbing you again. As you become free and continue these extra circles, back away from the attacker. Then run for help. An attacker will not pursue the child, but will move on to look for an easier child to abduct.

Only the thumb is holding the wrist.

When teaching this technique, be aware of two things. First, by reversing the circular flow, the child has added the strength of the attacker to their own because the attacker will have automatically tried to return their arm to its original position of control. Therefore, it is important for the child to move their arm in one direction with a quick motion and then reverse the circle in the other direction just as quickly. Second, do not allow the child to pull the attacker onto them. This strengthens the attacker's grip and reduces the effectiveness of the circular motion.

Throat Grab

A single-hand throat grab is a common assault grab used against children and women. An attacker uses a throat grab to gain control over a person and to impose a state of fear. When grabbed by the throat, a common reaction is to become rigid and unresponsive because the subconscious mind is searching for a response to restore normal breathing. The conscious mind interprets the situation as a helpless one and registers fear.

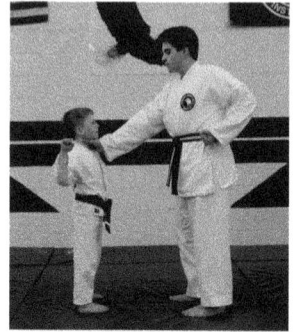

1) The Throat Grab

You can do something. The solution to this dilemma and feeling of helplessness is to arm the mind with the knowledge of how to free yourself in this situation.

Make a proper fist with the same arm as the person who has grabbed you. For example, if you are grabbed by the attacker's right arm, counter with your own right arm. Hold your forearm vertical so the fist is directly above your elbow. The fist should be about shoulder height and your arm should be bent. Rotate your upper body and strike the inside of the attacker's forearm near their elbow. As you strike the attacker's arm, turn your head slightly in the same direction as the strike. As this frees you from the attacker's grab, you should continue turning in the same direction, and run to a populated area. A child should then tell a helper or parent.

2) Strike Inside the Forearm

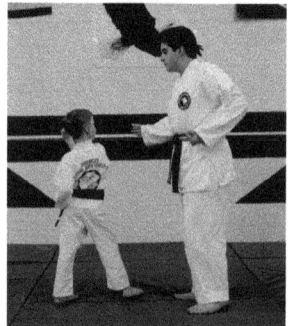

3) Step with the Strike

It is important to strike the forearm on the side of thumb, allowing less grabbing by the attacker as the block drives the attacker's arm from the throat.

4) Turn and Run for Help

Defensive Center Kick

For an attacker to grab a child, he must be close. Typically, he will need to bend down to reach the child because the difference in heights. This puts the attacker's knee close enough for the child to reach. The fact that the attacker is grabbing the child actually helps the child's balance while doing this technique.

Some children may need to be told where the shin is and that a kick to the shin looks funny on television, but it can really hurt. Also, keep in mind that if your son or daughter is very young, they may not have the strength or self-confidence to kick very hard. The practice you make available to them will change that. This kick can hurt a potential child molester and startle them, giving your child the chance to run for help.

1) Practicing the center kick with constant encouragement will help your son or daughter gain the confidence to make the kick effective.

2) You can practice using a shield, couch cushion, or pillow.

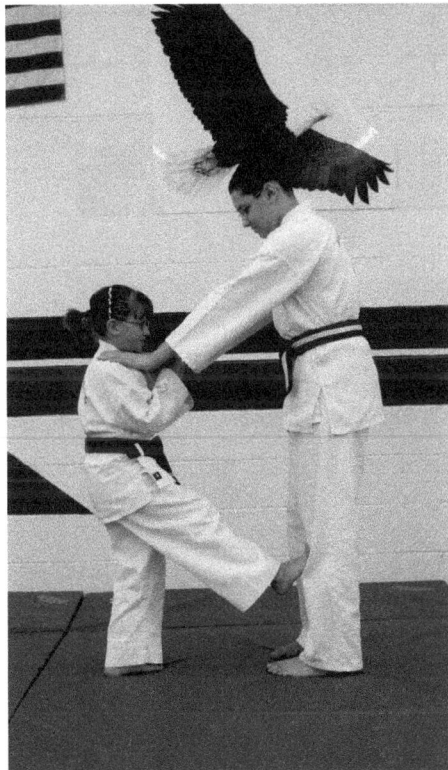

The kick to the knee or shin.

Executing the Kick:

The back leg executes the kick. Raise the knee upwards as high as possible to the front of the body. At this point, the foot should be directly under the knee with the toes pulled back and the ball of the foot extended downwards. This practice is best done barefoot. Extend the leg, penetrating with the foot in a forward motion until the knee is locked, and strike the target with the ball of the foot. The strike can impact anywhere from three inches above to three inches below the knee area of the attacker for maximum effect. The child should practice recocking the leg in a reverse motion with the understanding that they may need to kick again.

1) Stand with a guard.

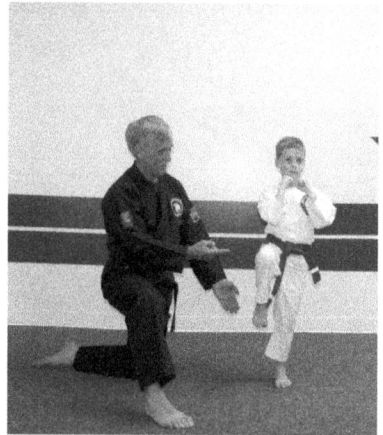

2) Raise your knee high.

3) Lock the leg out in front of you.

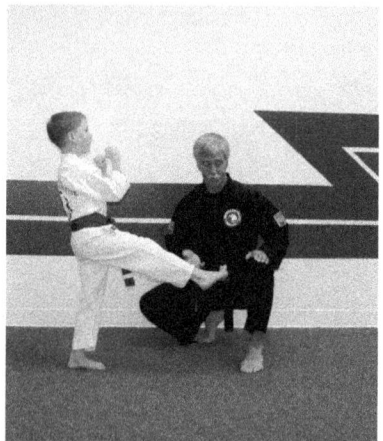

Side View

Responsive Move to Being Picked Up (Bear Hug)

An attacker may try to overpower a child by picking them up from behind. This is a challenging technique. The attacker must drop the child for them to escape; therefore, time needs to be taken to make the child feel safe about falling to the floor. Safety for the practice partner also becomes a major concern. The success of the technique will be based on the response time of the child.

Once picked up, the child should immediately begin striking backward with their heels in an attempt to impact the attacker's knees, upper thighs, or groin. These strikes should be done repeatedly, alternating between the left and right heels, until the child is dropped.

1) The child is picked up.

Simultaneously, the child should be striking backward with the back of their head, attempting to impact the face of the attacker. Once dropped, the child must get up immediately and run for help. When picked up, most children become rigid and literally hang there in fear and confusion. This state of vulnerability can be overcome by practice with this situation.

2) Kick backward with your heels repeatedly.

4) Be prepared to be dropped, and run for safety.

3) Strike backwards with the back of the head into the face.

LEVEL TWO Teenager's
Self-Defense & Social Awareness

The need for safety and awareness is important for people of all ages. Teenagers and adults have more independence than children, which provides the opportunity to participate in such activities as driving a car, visiting a foreign country, or buying a home. However, that independence also introduces new areas of vulnerability. Awareness and proactive safety practices can make the difference in living a more secure life.

Each level of the Crandall System is a progression toward secure living. The knowledge from previous levels establishes a foundation for the next. Therefore, it is beneficial to review level one before proceeding to level two. Level two presents subject areas for young adults between 13 and 19 years old. Depending on the maturity of the individual, some of this information may be relevant for a child younger than 13 years old. All of this information remains relevant for young adults as they enter into college and the work force, and it continues to be beneficial for adults throughout their lives. You need to possess the maturity and insight to incorporate the following information into your life to the best of your ability. Parents should go over these segments and present them to the young adults in their family in a format that best meets their children's intelligence and understanding.

Section One:
Socially Acceptable Responses

As a young adult, you face a complex challenge, learning how to make good, responsible decisions while achieving independence. This requires you to form a sense of identity, a firm and coherent understanding of yourself and what you want to do with your life. It also involves understanding how you fit into your community and society. You confront this complex challenge every day, and the decisions you make shape whom you are. This section focuses on peer pressure and makes suggestions on ways to gain control of your own life and decisions.

Peer Pressure

Being part of a group has many benefits. For example, you are less likely to be singled out by a potential bully, mugger, or rapist. A group of friends empowers you with the social self-confidence to make good decisions when you meet others for the first time. Being part of a group can make you feel important, loved, respected, and secure. The challenge of being part of a group is developing and maintaining your own identity. Despite all of the benefits a group affords, the reality is that they also have the potential to inflict harm and contribute to unsafe behaviors. While the group provides security, a group that makes poor decisions can put you at risk. It is important to understand that a group is a useful social tool, a means to increased safety, but like any tool, used improperly it can be harmful. A group is like a coin. It has two sides with pros and cons. When a group no longer works to improve your security and positive development, it loses

Your actions should be based on what you believe is right, not the group around you.

its value as a social tool, and at that time you should reevaluate your involvement with the group.

Sometimes you must decide to disagree with the group. Sometimes you must take a stand. Your actions should be based on what you believe is right, not the group around you. True friends will respect you for the strength of your convictions and your individuality. In time, they may even look to you as a leader, someone with the strength to impact their own life and the wisdom to make suggestions for the group. Every time you take a stand for what you believe, it becomes easier for you to do so the next time, and your friends become more understanding that that is who you are. However, saying, "no," to a group of peers can be one of the hardest actions you take. It can even be frightening. The power of peer pressure can feel overwhelming. To make a decision that is not considered the group norm takes tact and a clear understanding of why you're doing it. Here's something you may not realize. The test your peers give you to make the right choice does not only occur in elementary or high school. This peer pressure is something your parents, teachers, and different people of all professions deal with every day of their lives. If you forfeit choices you know are right simply because the group is applying peer pressure, you may only follow groups for your entire life and lose your individuality. To make a mistake is human, but to have as your only reason for making a mistake, "everyone else was doing it," is to surrender your future and dreams to others. Make good decisions that you can support with good reasons.

Socially Acceptable Responses

When friends question your decisions, it helps to have some socially acceptable responses to support your position. Socially acceptable responses defend your choice to be different in a way that is logical and consistent with how many other people behave, even if they are not part of your group. For example, many adults choose not to consume alcohol. It may be hard for others to understand why an adult who is legally old enough to drink would choose not to. A socially acceptable response in this situation could be, "I am in training, and I don't drink when I train." As a martial artist, runner, or other athlete, taking care of your body is socially recognized as being important, and athletes are valued in our society. This response explains your stance, which may be contrary to the group but is also acceptable.

Socially acceptable responses are useful in many other situations. If someone calls your house while you are alone, you should never say that you are alone. Instead, you can tell the caller that a family member is running late and you expect them home any minute. If they call back, that is normal, but if they call repeatedly, you can take a socially acceptable stand by saying, "I expect them home any minute, they are running late, and I don't want you to call again because you may tie up the phone if they are trying to reach me."

The number of situations where you may feel pressured by another person is vast. It helps to think about these situations before they arise so that you are mentally prepared to defend your stance. Remember, you are not alone. Every day millions of people stand up for what they believe in. Also, realize that peer pressure is not always negative. As a positive role model, you can influence your group to make good decisions and keep each other safe. Talk with your parents about some socially acceptable responses for different situations. Make your feelings and opinions consistently known with your peers. If your friends cannot accept your choices, then that is their problem, and you may be forced to acknowledge that they are not the friends you thought them to be. The thought of being without those friends may be scary, but if it means you retain the qualities that make you a self-confident individual in control of your own life and future, then it is a decision you may need to make.

Section Two:
Awareness for Teenagers

Accepting Rides

As children, you learned that riding with strangers is dangerous. That advice might seem like it only pertains to small children because as a young adult, you have more experience making decisions and you understand the dangers of riding with a stranger. Understand, getting into a car with a group of older students that you may have only met once or twice from another school is just as risky. Even riding with a friend of your boyfriend or girlfriend who graduated a year or two before can be dangerous. Sometimes who you

If you don't personally know them, don't get into the car with them.

should accept a ride from becomes an area that is gray with uncertainty. If you take a moment to think about the situation and get a bad feeling, then you should heed that feeling; it's a warning.

Where people make their greatest error in judgment is when they are close to home and feel safe. For example, if you are caught in the rain and become cold and sopping wet, it is tempting to accept a ride. After all, you can see your street only two blocks away. A short ride couldn't hurt. Right? Wrong. Once you enter their car, you leave your world and enter theirs. You are no longer in control, and they are free to drive you far away from your home. Though you may be uncomfortable, it is best to walk the remainder. Another tempting scenario is if your car breaks down or runs out of gas. A short ride home may seem harmless, but you should not relax your guard. Even if it is dark and snowing outside, it is still safer to use a cell phone and wait for help that you know or walk the remainder. Remember to follow the guidelines. If you don't personally know them, don't get into the car with them.

Costume Parties

Halloween can be a lot of fun for people of all ages. Many people enjoy wearing costumes, and teenagers and adults often look forward to costume parties, but holidays are not an excuse to do things that could put you in harm's way. A fun event can easily turn into a tragedy if you are not aware of your surroundings. Here is some advice to make costumes both fun and safe. First, your costume should be visible to drivers at night. For example, dressing in an all black ninja costume makes you indistinguishable from the darkness. The fact that drivers are looking at the variety of colorful costumes makes you even less noticeable and puts you at risk for an accident. Second, your costume should not overly restrict your movement and balance. This puts you at greater risk for assault and reduces your ability to react effectively in a defense situation. Also, be aware that if a fire or other emergency required you to quickly evacuate a building, you would have great difficulty. Finally, your costume should not restrict your senses so that you are less aware of the events around you. A mask that limits your vision or hearing may not be a good choice. These precautions, however, do not need to be taken to the extreme. If your costume is elaborate and limiting, then you can compensate for this vulnerability by using the buddy system. By having someone who can look out for you, drive for you if your costume reduces your visual range, and lead you around potential hazards, you can still enjoy the holiday and be safe. Allowing someone you trust to take some responsibility for your well being can give you more freedom in choosing your favorite costume. Enjoy the tradition of Halloween and costume parties, but dress defensively.

Keep in Contact

As a young adult, you may wish to be more independent, and the safety you used when you were younger may seem immature at first. Keep in mind that a businessman or woman keeps in constant contact with their office. They remain in contact with their home and family when they are on long trips. It is not only for safety and accountability, but it is courteous. Therefore, it is very important to take the time to tell your parent where you are going to be. If you decide to go somewhere else with a group of friends, call and update your parents about your plans or leave a message. Remember, your parents care about you, and they worry when they do not know where you are. The courtesy you give is the same as the courtesy you wish to receive from others.

The Buddy System

No matter what your age, it's good sense not to be alone in your exploration of the world around you. A small child should not play alone on the playground. If you have a younger brother or sister, you can tell them several good reasons why they should use the buddy system. An adult on vacation who has the opportunity to travel with another adult receives some additional benefits from traveling with another person. If they become sick unexpectedly, they may need help. If they get lost, they will be able to work together to find the help they need. It can be a lot of fun to go to the mall, attend a high school dance, or watch a rival school's football game. If you go with a friend, you will feel more secure. Having a friend gives you the social self-confidence to make good decisions when you meet new people, as mentioned earlier.

Weapons Carry with them Responsibility

There are many tools in our society that can be used as weapons. Many martial artists enjoy practicing with traditional extension tools such as the

tonfa, sai, kama, and sword because they provide a good cardiovascular workout, develop control and coordination, and are part of a rich traditional heritage of the marital arts. Guns can be used for recreational shooting on a range and require great skill and focus. Knives can be used in hunting, carving wood, preparing food, and as safety tools such as cut-away knives for skydiving and scuba diving. Bows and arrows are popular for target shooting and hunting, as well. These

Some knives used for carving, preparing food, and other household chores.

tools carry with them responsibility and should never be taken to school or in public places like parks and playgrounds. Taking these weapons out of their proper context often results in accidents or injury. Using these tools can be an opportunity to improve your physical skills and to enjoy socially appropriate activities.

Safeguard your Bicycles

Bicycle riding is good exercise and a lot of fun. It can also be a means of transportation, allowing you to get to and from school, a friend's house, a mall, or other activities. Safeguarding your bicycle from possible theft takes only a moment, and it is worth it if it discourages a thief. Here are some things you can do.

> **First**, make a mark somewhere on your bike that only you know about that will help you identify it if it is lost and later found.
> **Second**, have a name or ID number engraved on the bike somewhere.
> **Lastly**, use a bike lock, either the padlock or chain type, and take the time to secure your bike before you leave it unattended.

These steps may make the difference between you riding or walking home.

Say NO to Steroids

This book encourages a safe and secure life, and it was written to establish a broader base of common sense. With that in mind, realize there are many ways to damage your physical and mental health. Some of these methods come disguised as ways to benefit your health or appearance. In reality, they are harmful. One method of altering appearance and body structure is steroids. Do not use steroids unless a doctor has prescribed them as medicine for your general health. Certain steroids occur in the body naturally like cholesterol and hormones, and doctors may prescribe them if we are lacking the ones we need.

If you take steroids just to change your appearance, size, shape, or even athletic abilities, then you are missing the point of who you are and what you can accomplish naturally. Steroids in weight lifting, football, baseball, and many other activities create a body that is artificial and unstable. When you take steroids, your accomplishments are artificial, as well. Your body becomes like a balloon blown up beyond its capacity, just waiting to explode. The damage to internal organs, like your kidneys and spleen, make steroids a drug that harms. Do some investigation. To learn more about the uses and abuses of steroids, check at the library, talk with your doctor, or simply go online.

Technology, Internet Use, and Identity

Every generation faces unique challenges to their safety and security. The rapid development of new technologies is both amazing and challenging. The development of the cellular phone has allowed people to keep in better contact with one another and be prepared to seek help in emergencies. If a car breaks down today, you are no longer isolated and dependent on the kindness of a stranger to stop and assist you. You can call for help. Unfortunately, if you are home alone and a stranger calls you, you can no longer simply tell them that your parents or friends are in the next room but unavailable. A potential assailant could be calling from a cellular phone, watching your house as they talk with you, and they know you are alone. Through socially acceptable responses and awareness, you can reduce your risk as a target. Level four of the

Be cautious when dealing with strangers online.

Crandall System addresses additional precautions that can be taken to safeguard your house against an intruder.

While new technology can improve our lives, there will always be people who exploit it for criminal actions. It is important to maintain an open mind throughout your entire life and learn about new technologies as they become mainstream, but it is equally important to use the technology responsibly to remain safe.

The Internet is perhaps the most powerful information tool in modern society. It instantly connects you to people all over the world. It is important to learn about the wide variety of chat rooms, blogs, message boards, and personal WebPages. Remember that the rules for dealing with strangers are just as important online as it is in person or over the telephone. Not everyone online is honest, and there is no way for you to verify his or her identity. The information they provide, including pictures of themselves, their friends, and their family, may not be genuine.

Every year, child molesters, rapists, kidnappers, and other criminals go online and impersonate a friendly person to gain the confidence and friendship of someone they don't know. They feel like a real, genuine friend, but you have never met them. You wouldn't and shouldn't meet with a new friend or date for the first time unless it is in a public place with other people and friends that you do know. Never agree to meet someone alone that you have only communicated with over the Internet.

Avoid giving out information that could assist a criminal in assaulting you. Your full name, pictures, address, and other information should be kept private. The personal information you post online can be read by anyone. It is also good to note that any personal information that goes online may stay online for years. Don't feel as if these preventative measures are paranoia or an overreaction. Most of the time, the people you meet online are good people like yourself. Remember, good relationships build slowly over time between people as they interact and develop trust.

Driving

One of the most exciting times in the life of a young adult is learning how to drive. While it is an important step along the path to independence, it is also a serious responsibility. You should realize that driving a car opens up new areas of vulnerability in your life. There are people who will want to rob you, steal your stereo, airbag, and other car parts, or hijack your entire car. Your car will take you to places with which you are unfamiliar. Driving a car creates new areas for awareness that you should practice for your own personal safety. Here are some things to consider when you start driving.

Always Wear Your Seatbelt

Wearing a seatbelt is a logical safeguard to prevent or minimize injuries in an accident, but it can also assist in self-defense during a hijacking situation. When someone gets into the passenger seat and threatens you with a weapon such as a knife, they will not take the precaution of buckling their seatbelt. This allows you to drive your car into a stationary object like a tree, parked car, pole, *et cetera*. Your mental preparedness and seatbelt will protect you. The assailant will impact the dashboard or

Hitting a stationary object may allow you to escape.

windshield. This allows you to leave the car and flee for help. The accident will also draw attention of bystanders, the police, and fire officials. Insurance claims are a better choice over hospital bills and injuries.

Footwear

How you dress also affects your ability to react and drive defensively. A young woman who is dressed for a special occasion should wear sensible footwear and bring her high-heeled shoes with her. If you need to brake quickly to avoid an accident, heels make it more likely that your foot will slip and you will lose control of the car.

Don't Limit Your Senses

Whether you are driving a car, riding a motorcycle, or riding a bicycle, personal alertness and good self-defense is dependent on all of your senses. Don't limit your awareness by listening to music so loud that you cannot hear the world around you. As a new driver, you already know that the road is a constantly changing environment, and, as a result, you can't always see everything around you. To compensate for this limitation, you rely more heavily on your other senses. You need to be able to hear an ambulance, fire truck, or police car's siren. You need to be able to hear a warning beep from a horn of someone pulling out of his or her driveway. You need to be able to hear your friend's warning from the back seat if they spot a small child running out into the road after a ball. Wearing headphones while driving or listening to music at extreme volumes overly occupies your brain to deal with sounds, and you lose sight of some things. Limiting your senses can lead to an accident that puts others at risk for injury or even death. Enjoy the privilege of driving and the independence that it offers, but don't limit your senses. Drive safely.

The Emotional State of Other Drivers

It is important to abide by the laws when you drive. The primary purpose is to prevent vehicular accidents on the road, but it is also important when you consider the emotional states of other drivers. Getting into an accident could not only result in harming yourself, your passengers, and others, but it could also anger the other driver and result in a physical assault. Someone you cut off in traffic could follow you until your next stop at a gas station, the mall, or your own home, and, in their anger over what they believe you did to them on the road, they may assault you. Most situations that require physical responses can be avoided by awareness and prevention. Keep those situations in mind when you drive. Realize, you cannot know the state of mind of other drivers.

Running or Walking

If you wear headphones and listen to music when you walk or run, you should be able to hear the traffic and world around you. Your awareness is your first defense against an assault. Limiting your hearing may prevent you from noticing the warning sounds of an attacker approaching, a car backing out of a driveway, or even a dog running fast on your heels. This can result in personal injury or death. If you wear headphones, you can take some precautions. There are many kinds of earphones. The kind that insert into the ear make it very easy to wear just one and tuck the other into your shirt. Some earphones are connected by a wire over the head and can be worn with one off one ear or just in front of both ears. Use all of your senses to remain aware of your surroundings.

Section Three:
Escape Techniques

Being a Good Partner When Practicing Self-Defense

When practicing self-defense, it is just as important for the partner to be helpful as it is for the practitioner to execute the technique properly. As in level one, self-defense requires self-confidence. Self-defense works because of the element of surprise. When you respond in a way that an attacker does not anticipate, your chances for escaping the situation are great. Learning self-defense so that it becomes an automatic response requires repetition. Just like memorizing any school subject, rote memorization arms the subconscious mind with the skills for the body to react. However, during practice, this repetition eliminates the element of surprise for your self-defense partner. Remember, an attacker does not know what motions the defender will make; therefore, resisting your partner because you can prevent the technique from working is unrealistic and only serves to erode their self-confidence. Also, remember that an attacker does not grab you with all of their possible strength. Their attention is divided between the physical attack and watching their surroundings to make certain they have not been seen, and this decreases the strength of the grab. Sometimes as partners, it is tempting to try to resist a technique in the mistaken belief that this will simulate a more realistic situation. Avoid this temptation.

Students Should Review the Following Level One Techniques:

1. Circular Arm Breakaway   2. Single Handed Throat Grab

These level two techniques are illustrated for an attacker using a particular grab. Please remember to practice the techniques for both your left and right sides of your body.

Straight-Across Wrist Grab

The attacker's right arm grabs your left arm.

Down Block Technique

1) The Straight Across Wrist Grab

Close your right hand into a proper fist and raise it to your left shoulder. Step back with your left foot, moving away from the attacker's arm that has grabbed you. Slide your right arm down your left arm as hard as you can, striking the assailant's wrist, and simultaneously pull your left arm back. At this point, you have two choices. You can flee from the area and get help, or you can follow this freeing motion with a counterstrike to the attacker.

2) Bring your right arm to your left shoulder.

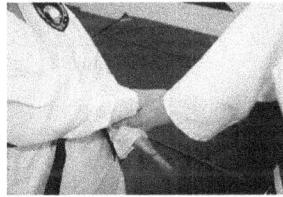

Close-up of the impact.

3) Execute the down block.

4) You are free to escape.

Straight Breakaway

The attacker uses a straight across wrist grab to grab your right wrist with his left hand. Open your right hand so the fingers are extended but together. This increases the circumference of your wrist by expanding the forearm muscles and helps to weaken the attacker's grip. At this point, turn your open hand palm towards the floor. Bring you right hand to your left shoulder quickly with force and speed, and step back with your left foot, rotating at the waist. This motion results in bending your right arm at the elbow and driving that elbow into the back the attacker's left forearm. Once your wrist is free from the grasp of the attacker's fingers and thumb, you can continue turning your body and run from the situation.

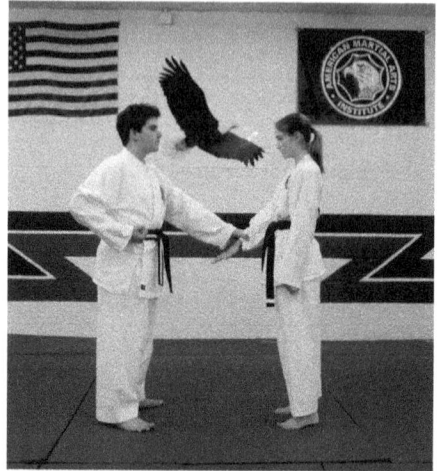

1) The straight across wrist grab.

2) Step back and bring your open hand to your shoulder.

Cross Wrist Grab Close-up:

1) The cross wrist grab.

2) Grab the attacker's wrist by making a small circle with your hand.

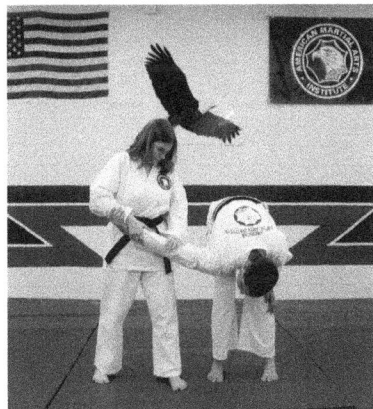

3) Step in and place your hand to the back of the attacker's elbow.

Cross Wrist Grab

The attacker's right arm grabs your right arm.

Reverse Grip Arm Control

Bring your right hand up to about shoulder height with your elbow directly underneath your wrist, and rotate your forearm so the palm of your right hand grabs the attacker's right wrist. Step forward and slightly to the right with your left foot so your body is angled and your left foot is between you and the attacker. While your left foot is stepping forward, place your left hand on the elbow of the attacker's right arm. Pull your right hand, which is holding the attacker's wrist, up to your chest, and push down with your left hand, which is on the back of the attacker's elbow. This puts the attacker off balance and leaves them vulnerable. If you quickly step back with your right foot and twist your upper body clockwise, the attacker will fall face down to the floor. At this point, let go and run to a safe place.

4) The takedown.

53

Shoulder Grab

The attacker reaches out with his left arm and grabs your right shoulder.

Lock and Takedown

1) Grab the attacker's hand, and place your forearm on the outside of the attacker's arm.

Reach up with your left hand, grab the attacker's right hand that is on your shoulder, and press it firmly into your shoulder so that it is locked to your body. Bend your right arm slightly and raise it up to the outside of the attacker's arm. As your arm rises, the forearm applies pressure against the attacker's elbow and rolls his arm over so that the attacker's arm is locked straight, his elbow is pointing to the ceiling, and the thumb of his hand, which you are still holding to your shoulder, points downward. Step back with your left foot away from the attacker. Simultaneously, push straight down with your right arm on the attacker's elbow, trying to bring your forearm toward your body. This will bring the attacker to his knees on the floor so that you are free let go and flee.

2) Roll the attacker's arm over and press down.

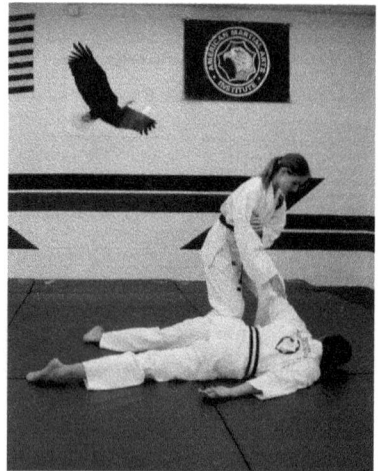

3) Take the attacker to the ground.

Double-Handed Throat Grab

The attacker places both hands around your throat.

By squaring off their shoulders, the attacker has made it possible for you to reach out and strike or simply push into the soft area of their throat. This technique works using either your left or right arm singularly. Keep your fingers together and cup your hand. Turn your shoulders and extend your arm straight between the attacker's arms and impact their throat area with the arc of your hand between your thumb and cupped fingers.

1) The Double Throat Grab

2) Step forward and strike into the throat with an open arc hand.

Alternatively, use a spear hand to the throat by keeping your fingers together.

Sleeve Grab

The attacker grabs you by the sleeve area of your coat somewhere between the elbow and shoulder area.

Lock and Takedown

Swing your arm in front of your body and up in a circular motion. When your arm is about chest height, step in toward your attacker and turn your body so that your right hip is perpendicular to theirs (they are facing forward and you are facing their right side). Continue to swing your arm up and over their arm. As your arm comes down behind theirs, you will have created a bend in their elbow. Bend your arm at the elbow so your hand is palm up with your forearm directly beneath the bend of their elbow. Push upward. This locks their shoulder joint,

1) The Sleeve Grab

controls their elbow, and stretches the muscles that cover the rib cage. You now have two choices. Place your left palm on the shoulder joint that is locked, step around with your left foot to face into the technique, and push down on the shoulder joint while rotating at the waist. This will throw the assailant to the floor. Alternatively, if you chose to swing your arm through the area between your body with the proper power and speed, you can dislocate your attacker's shoulder.

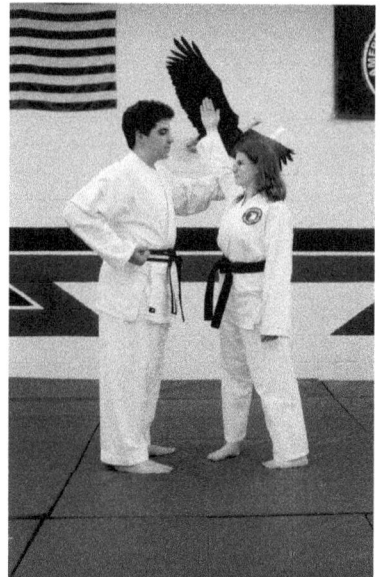

2) Step in and swing your arm up and over their arm.

3) Push upward under the attacker's elbow.

4) Step in and place your hand on the attacker's shoulder.

Closeup from another angle of the hand on the shoulder just prior to the takedown.

5) Push down on the shoulder joint to complete the takedown.

The takedown from another angle.

Double Lapel Grab

The attacker uses both hands to grab the front of your coat or shirt and curls the material into his hands.

If you cannot reach the attacker's head, step forward. Reach around the back of the attacker's head with your left hand and cup the base of their skull near their left ear. Reach across the front of your body with your right hand and place the palm of your hand at the base of the attacker's right jaw and cheek. The attacker's head should be pressed between your two hands. Step back with your left foot and rotate at the waist. At the same time, turn the attacker's head counterclockwise by pushing their jaw with your right hand and pulling at the base of their skull with your left hand. The attacker will fall to the ground allowing you to escape. Be aware that a fast twisting motion here could break the cervical vertebrae of the neck.

1) A double lapel grab.

2) Reach around to the base of the skull with your left hand and place your right hand to the attacker's right jaw.

A close-up of the hand position on the head as they are set up to complete the takedown.

3) Step back with your left foot and rotate the attacker's head to bring them to the floor.

View from a different angle of the completed takedown. Notice the hands still in control of the head.

Single Lapel Grab

The attacker uses one hand to grab the front of your coat or shirt and curls the material into his hand.

Place your right forearm on the attacker's forearm. Your right arm should be bent at the elbow so that it is parallel with your chest and forms a right angle to the attacker's arm. Grab your right wrist with your left hand. The left hand should be palm down. Step back from the attacker and bring your arms down to your body sharply. Keep the right angle arm structure as you complete this technique.

1) A single lapel grab.

3) Grab your right wrist.

2) Place your right forearm on the attacker's forearm.

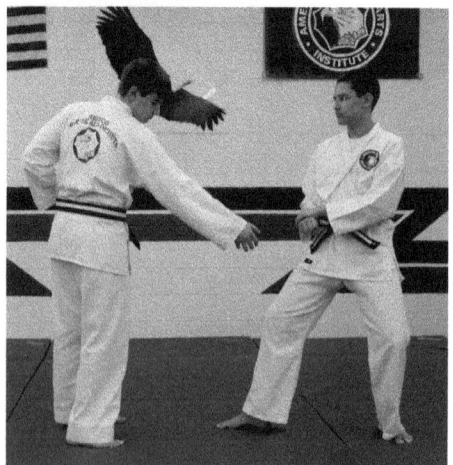

4) Step back and bring your arms down to your body sharply to get free.

Hair Grab

First, the attacker's hand needs to be locked into a controlled spot. This is done by using both your hands, one on top of the other, to grab and hold the attacker's hand in your hair and on the top of your head.

Hair Grab from the Front

If the attacker is facing you and has grabbed your hair with his right hand, you would respond by stepping forward with your right foot so that it will land just beyond the attacker's arm to his right side. You will then dip down and go under the attacker's arm, still clenching his attack hand to the top of your head. Once the right foot has stabilized, you pivot counter-clockwise, bringing your left foot now through the space between the attacker's feet and your right foot. The left foot will cease its movement when it reaches a central area directly behind the attacker. At this point, you push your head into the attacker's back, and stand up as tall as possible. This will lock the attacker's arm, wrenching his shoulder and elbow as his hand is pushed up closer to the base of his neck. You now release the grip with your left hand and grab his hair. Your right hand maintains control of the wrist and hand of the attacker and you step back, pulling him off balance and taking control.

1) The hair grab from the front.

2) Grab the attacker's hand and secure it tightly to your head.

3) Step to the attacker's right side by moving your right foot and go under their arm.

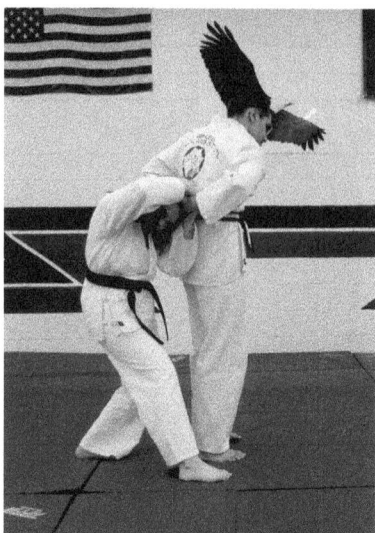

4) Step behind the attacker by moving your left foot and begin to stand up

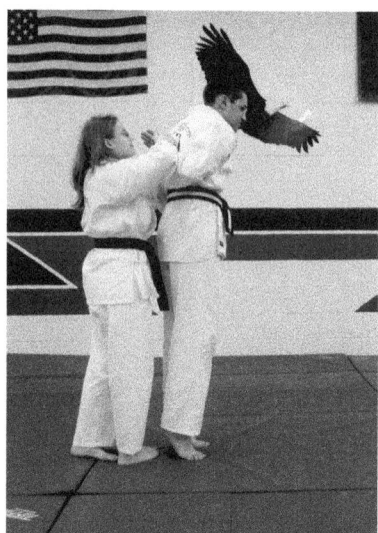

5) Stand up and take control of the attacker.

Hair Grab from Behind

If the attacker grabs you from behind, lock the attacker's hand to your head by grabbing them as you did in the hair grab from the front. Bend your knees, dip down, and pivot around so that you are facing the attacker in a crouched position. Hold their hand to your head tight and stand straight up. The attacker's palm should face to the ceiling. Kick to the knee or let go and run away.

1) The hair grab from behind.

2) Grab the attacker's hand

3) Dip down, pivot around and hold onto their hand tightly.

4) Stand straight up and kick to the knee.

Arm Around the Shoulder

1) Arm around the shoulder.

The attacker places their left arm around your shoulder in an effort to pull you in towards them. You will use your right arm in defense by bringing it down between yourself and the attacker and moving it in a circular motion back between yourself and the attacker. As it rises, you should bend your elbow, bringing your right forearm down on the shoulder or upper section of the attacker's left arm. Simultaneously, you now place your right foot behind the attacker's left foot, and extend your right arm out as far as possible. The straightening of your right arm should result in the palm of your right hand being pressed backwards into the attacker's throat or chin. By continuing the pressure and the pushing of your right hand back, the attacker will fall over your right foot, losing his control and landing on the ground.

2) Step back behind their leg and swing your arm up overhead from behind the attacker.

3) Bring the hand down to the chin or throat.

Close-up of the hand position prior to completing the takedown.

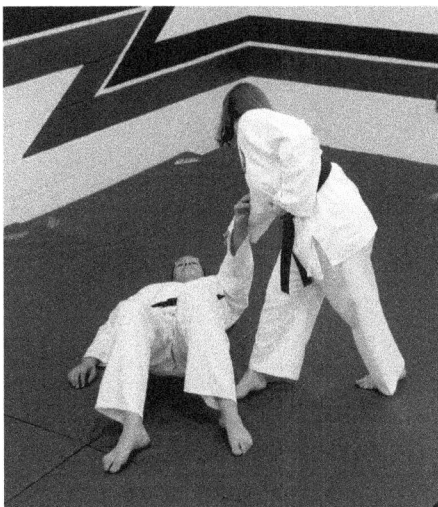

4) Straighten your arm to take them down. Note: This picture is from another angle.

Arm around the Waist

If an aggressor places his hand around your waist and does not remove it after you firmly tell them to take their hands off you, the following

technique will be very effective. The attacker has used their left arm. Swing your right arm up in front of you to your right until it is above your shoulder and between yourself and the aggressor. It should now be brought down behind you and the attacker and firmly straightened so your arm becomes rigid. Continue bringing this rigid arm down and move your right foot slightly forward and to the left. As you take this step, your right arm will come in contact with the back of the attacker's elbow of his left arm. The amount of pressure and speed at which your arm is brought in contact with the attacker's will determine the amount or level of injury that will occur to the attacker.

1) Arm around the waist.

2) Swing your arm overhead.

3) Bring your arm down behind the elbow, keeping your arm locked.

4) Step back with your left foot and push on the arm for a takedown.

The takedown from another angle. Notice that the attacker's arm is locked and under control.

Rear Choke Hold

1) Choke hold from behind.

The attacker grabs you from behind with their right arm going over your right shoulder and encircling your throat. Turn your upper body slightly to the left, away from the crook of their elbow. Then quickly twist your upper body back to the right. This will create an area of space and movement, which will now allow you to swing your right arm up and behind the attacker. At this point, with your right hand, you should grasp the hair of the attacker or the collar structure of the coat or shirt the attacker is wearing. At the same time, you should now place your right foot out approximately eight to twelve inches to the side and use your right arm to pull the attacker's head down and around in front of you. The attacker will stumble over your sidestepped right foot and fall on his back directly in front of you. At this point, you can flee the area.

2) Turn and grab the collar or hair of the attacker with your right arm, and grab the attacker's upper arm with your left arm.

3) Bring the attacker down in front of you.

4) The attacker will fall in front of you, and you are free to escape the situation.

Bear Hug

One of the scariest attack situations is being grabbed from behind. Understand that the attacker has committed all of his weapons to this action, leaving him very little else he can do. His feet are firmly planted on the ground in an effort to control your body and your unpredictable reaction to being grabbed. Both his hands and arms are committed to the bear hug hold itself. On the other hand, you have both your feet available to kick backward into the knee area or stomp down onto the attacker's toes. Your hands may be in position to grab onto one of the attacker's fingers and pull or twist it to become free. The back of your head is in a position to be moved backward repeatedly, which will most likely make contact with the aggressor's face area, resulting in you being let go to run.

You may also use the following escape technique. Step out with your left leg into a horse stance, dropping your center of gravity, and thrust both arms straight out in front of you as hard and fast as possible. This will result in the attacker's arms rising up to around your shoulders. Grab the attacker's right wrist with your left hand by reaching up between your body and their arm. Strike the attacker in the solar plexus with your elbow. This strike does two things. First, it spasms the lungs so they have they "have the wind knocked out of them." Second, the impact occupies their mind for a moment so they temporarily stop thinking about regrabbing you. Complete the technique by swinging your right arm between your body and theirs and placing your arm up on their right shoulder. Place your right knee on the ground, and push with your right hand as you pull with your left arm so they are thrown onto the ground in front of you. Run for safety.

1) The Bear Hug.

2) Step out and thrust arms forward.

3) Grab the attacker's arm and strike with your elbow.

4) Bring your arm behind the attacker and kneel.

5) Throw the attacker.

6) The attacker falls in front of you.

Defense Against a Punch

1) Block the punch.

2) Pivot around the attacker.

3) You are free to run.

Many times an attacker will grab you before attempting to punch you. In these situations, doing one of the escape techniques will both free you from the grab and prevent them from striking you. Awareness should prevent the situation where someone would try to punch you. Assault is usually preceded by escalating verbal attacks and aggressive body language. It is important not to add to these situations by becoming angry or aggressive. However, if someone attempts to punch you, there is something you can do.

The attacker punches with his left arm toward your head. Block the attack with a right outside block (consult page 155 for information on supporting materials to learn more about blocking). This technique is similar to the escape from a single throat grab. Make a proper fist. Keep the fist above the elbow and level with the shoulder. Bring this structure from the outside of your body and block into the outside the attacker's forearm. At the same time, step forward and to the right with your right leg. By going to the outside of their body and moving in you do two things. First, you deflect the punch. Second, you neutralize the effectiveness of a second punch because it cannot reach you. Continue this escape technique by pivoting around the attacker counterclockwise. This is done by stepping around with your left leg and turning your back to the attacker as you roll off their body. Now that you are behind the attacker, run for safety.

Women's Self-Defense & Assault Prevention

Level three of the Crandall System is intended for women 18 years and older. This information is beneficial for teenage girls, but parent supervision is recommended because of the mature nature of assault situations. The primary goal of this level is to heighten your awareness regarding the ways you can prevent physical assault and rape. It also deals with home intrusions and responses to physical conflicts.

Section One:
Awareness, Preventions, and Precautions

When put into practice, the information in this section can help you reduce your vulnerability, increase your awareness of your surroundings, and become more proactive in your daily life. If you take precautions to both mentally and physically prepare yourself for action, it may never be necessary to use the physical skills of self-defense. This knowledge is a foundation you should build upon as the first steps toward a more secure future.

10 Tips for Assault Prevention

The following suggestions regard measures to prevent assaults. Some of these tips are elaborated on in greater detail following this list.

1. Be alert to what is happening around you.

2. Be careful when dealing with people seeking directions, and keep your distance from their car.

3. If you are being followed by a car, turn around and walk the other way. Go up a one-way street if possible. Get the license plate number and a description of the car.

4. Before you walk out to your car, have your car keys in your hand. When entering your car, check the back seat and floor before getting in. After entering your car, lock the doors.

5. Don't hitchhike, pick up hitchhikers, or accept rides with strangers.

6. Report obscene phone calls to the police immediately.

7. Do not give information over the phone to people you do not know including calls for your husband, roommate, *et cetera.*

8. When in trouble, yell "Fire!"

9. Be mentally and physically prepared for any type of action.

10. Become proficient enough at self-defense to protect yourself if the need arises.

Tip #2: People Seeking Directions

If you become lost while driving, you can seek directions by driving to a well-populated area, but what should you do when someone in a car asks for your help? While most people seeking directions are in genuine need of help, it is always wise to exercise caution. A common method of abduction involves luring a person closer to the car by using a map and asking directions. Once you are close enough to be reached, they grab you and step on the accelerator. To avoid falling out of a moving car, you will unconsciously assist them in being pulled into the vehicle through the open window.

Getting too close allows the driver to pull you into the vehicle.

Keeping your distance keeps you in control of the situation, and it is much safer.

Also, be aware of what is going on around you when you are offering directions. Someone could come up from behind you while you are distracted. Keep your directions simple. The less time you are in contact with a stranger, the safer you are. In addition, simple directions will be more helpful to a lost driver, and they can always ask another for more directions when they are closer to their destination. If you cannot be heard, speak louder. Avoid going closer to the vehicle. Helping people is fine, but use caution while doing so.

Tip 3: Being Followed (the Identifying Look)

If you feel you are being followed by someone, there are several things you can do. First, acknowledge that warning signal inside you. Don't scold yourself. Don't consider yourself paranoid or foolish. If you feel you are being followed, check it out. Whether you are at a mall or on the street, you should stop, turn, and look at the person's face. This is called an identifying look. A potential assailant wants an easy victim that cannot identify them after the crime. When you make it clear that you could give the police a description, you deter their willingness to risk an assault. If you don't want to talk to them, don't give them any kind of verbal response, simply turn and see what they look like. Your facial expression should remain neutral, as well.

It is best to be direct, but you can be more subtle. Use a store's window reflection or a hand-sized mirror to check to see if you are being followed. If you believe that you're being followed, don't go to your car as a place of safety. It is often the least safe place because of its isolation. Instead, remain in a populated area.

Knowing your surroundings makes you less of a target. If you are traveling in an unfamiliar city or shopping at an out-of-town mall, stay with a group if possible. When you must travel alone, try to become familiar with the area in advance. You can become better acquainted by purchasing maps or utilizing the Internet's resources. Remain alert while shopping, and when you are done, it is perfectly acceptable to ask security to escort you to your car, as well.

The reflection of a store window may allow you to see if you are being followed.

What should you do if you feel someone is following your car? Drive into a populated area or a gas station. Drive to the police station. Don't drive home. Driving home tells that person where you live, and you may be alone. Remember, don't criticize yourself or feel you are being paranoid. Most of the time, you won't be in any danger, but if you ignore all of your feelings, you may ignore the wrong one.

Tip 4: Entering Your Car

When a criminal plans an assault, they choose a location that minimizes their risk of being seen and identified by others, and they assess a target's vulnerability. Therefore, many assaults occur in a parking lot while their target is preoccupied with shopping bags. Before you leave the store to walk out to your car, have your keys in your hand. While you search for your keys in a pocket or purse, you become less aware of your surroundings. Before you enter your car, look in the back seat and make certain that no one is hiding there. A dark parking lot allows an assailant to blend in. Once you are in your car, lock all of the doors immediately. This precaution prevents someone from opening your door and pulling you from your vehicle. It also stops them from getting in your passenger seat with a weapon. If someone does

Always check the back seat before entering your vehicle.

attempt to hijack your car at gunpoint, give them the car. It is not worth risking your life over unless your children or other people are in the car. Finally, never get in the car with the assailant.

Tips 6 and 7: The Telephone

Always report obscene phone calls to the police. Even if the call seems like it is only a childish prank, it is best to inform the authorities. You may be in no immediate physical danger, but criminal acts have a tendency to escalate when the perpetrator gains confidence. If the calls continue, the police will be able to assist you. It is important to document every incident immediately after it happens. The police can only respond to a situation within the confines of the law, and failure to report the incident the first time it occurs may later limit some of the protections the police could afford you. Your reporting of harassing calls may combine with other reports in your area and result in the police having a better chance of apprehending the perpetrator.

Do not give out information over the telephone. Telling someone that you are alone or that you are leaving your house unattended puts you at risk for assault. If you are alone and someone calls for your husband or roommate, tell them that you expect them home any minute. This indicates that you will not be alone long. You cannot simply lie and tell them that the person they are calling for is unavailable. The criminal could be calling from a cellular phone and watching you from outside your home while you talk. They may explain that they are a childhood friend or a salesperson who your husband or roommate spoke with earlier in the week. They may be telling the truth, but you cannot be sure. If they call back, and you are still alone, you can tell them that your husband or roommate is running late, but you expect them home and minute. Ask to take a message so they can be called back later, but also tell them not to call again because you don't want them to tie up the phone line in case your husband is trying to reach you. If after this they call again, it is appropriate to tell them that if they call again, you will call the police.

Tip 8: Yell "Fire"

Yelling, "help," during an emergency is an automatic reaction for most people. Unfortunately, the cry of "help" does not attract the attention it once did. Coming to your aid would put a helper at risk. Instead, they may call the police or go for professional help, but that is no guarantee that help will arrive quickly. The police are often already committed to dealing with another incident somewhere else in the town or city. The same is true for campus or building security guards. The time it will take them to respond could be only minutes, but it could also be much longer. In an emergency, it is more beneficial to yell "Fire!" People will come out to assess the danger of fire for their own personal safety before they will come out to stop an assailant. They will call the fire department or 911. The fire department is trained specifically to respond rapidly in these situations and is less likely to be committed to another incident. The attention of the sirens and multiple vehicles that will show up in the area, including police, is what you want. It will scare the assailant away. It is better to explain to the fire officials and police what happened than to be raped or killed. The key is to draw as much attention to you as possible to scare away the assailant.

Tips 9 and 10: Physical Actions

Your mind is the most powerful tool in the world. Your ability to take physical action resides in your mind's ability to control the body. In many respects, your mind is like a computer. Ask a computer to do something that it is not programmed to do and it will not respond. During a physical attack, your mind can become overwhelmed by the situation, flooded with emotions and information that needs to be processed. If your mind is not programmed with how to respond, the body may not react. When forced to defend against an assault, you must be prepared both mentally and physically. Learn how to defend yourself so that you can take action if the need arises. Becoming proficient in self-defense requires repetition and self-confidence. The more you practice, the more self-confident you will become. Through regular practice, you can arm your mind with the knowledge that may allow your body to respond to an attack. You do not need dozens of self-defense techniques, only a few effective ones. Learning and practicing the techniques in this book can make a difference.

Carrying a Weapon for Security

There are some things you should consider before relying on a weapon for your security. Carrying mace or a compression horn is not usually very practical. These devices give you an artificial sense of security and may actually cause you to relax your awareness of your surroundings. To be useful, they must also be readily accessible, and most often these items are stored in a purse where they may become confused with other items. Even if they are at hand, they may not even function properly in an emergency. During some Crandall System rape prevention classes, we tested a couple of these items. A 37-year-old woman in the class had carried a compression horn with her for over a year, but she hadn't dared to try it. Once the horn had gone off, she would have to replace it, and she didn't want everyone to come running during her test. We all stepped out on the sidewalk after class to see just how loud this gas-compressed horn really was. Grandmaster Crandall removed the cap and pushed the button. Nothing. Not a sound came out. For over a year this had been her first defense, and it didn't work. On another occasion we tried a canister of mace. It sprayed, but only about a foot to a foot-and-a-half. If there had been a breeze, it would have done little good. These examples do not mean that there aren't products that might assist you in a serious situation. The point is that your best defense resource is yourself. The knowledge in your mind is your resource for the potential action, awareness, and self-confidence to capitalize on any way to escape a situation.

Regarding the Purse

There is nothing in your purse worth your life and well being. Only fight when you are personally in danger and have no alternatives left. If you fear someone is following you and they intend to steal your purse, head for a populated area. When there isn't enough time to reach other people, you can safeguard your purse by dropping it into a federal

Throwing your purse at an attacker can create a moment when you can flee to safety.

mailbox or throwing it on top of a building for safety.

It is important to know what a criminal wants. Do they want you or your purse? You can determine this by throwing your purse in one direction and running in the opposite direction. If they ignore your purse and continue to pursue you, then you know they intend an assault and not simply a

1) She gives the assailant an identifying look.

robbery. However, if you are confronted face-to-face and believe they intend to harm you, your purse becomes a secondary concern. Now you

2) She throws the purse away and runs in the opposite direction.

use the purse to distract the individual by throwing it straight at them. The purse becomes an obstacle they must avoid, and it creates a moment when you can run to get free.

What should you do if your purse is grabbed unexpectedly, and the assailant tries to wrestle it from you? Try not to use your energy to maintain control over the purse. Instead, try to open the purse and spill its contents onto the ground. The wallet is probably what the thief wants, and they

may now pick it up and run away, leaving you with your car keys, driver's license, and other valuables. In securing yourself, use what you have available wisely.

3) She runs to a populated area, and the criminal steals the purse and flees.

Precautionary Steps Regarding Your Purse:

A purse is an excellent way to carry a variety of items that you may need when you shop or travel. However, carrying a purse creates a target, and you should consider taking some precautions.

1. Don't put all of your money in your purse. Put some in your coat or pants pocket, as well.

2. Don't carry all of your credit cards with you. Take only the ones with you that you feel you will need for what you are doing. All of your credit cards are not needed to pick up some groceries.

3. Keep your driver's license or credit cards in a small wallet or folder separate from your money wallet.

Dressing Appropriately

There are many occasions for you to dress up. You may be meeting somebody, shopping at the mall, running an errand at the store, or sightseeing at a nearby city. Whatever your purpose for going out, it should have a direct influence on your choice of dress. If you are meeting a close friend, someone special, or a business acquaintance, you will probably dress in some of the more current fashions and styles. Unfortunately, most of these fashions limit what they permit you to do to defend yourself, and they often create challenges for simple balance. You can compensate for these limitations in a number of ways. For example, keep a comfortable pair of shoes in your car for when you are done or return to your car with a friend.

When you go shopping, it is obvious to everyone watching you that you are carrying your money and credit cards. When visiting and shopping in large cities, such as New York, Los Angeles, Chicago, or Dallas, you are easy to identify as a tourist. Criminals know that you are carrying money, are unfamiliar with the area, and won't know where to go for help. Like most people, when you are searching for that special gift or an unusual bargain, you are seldom aware of people who may intend to steal your purse or to assault you when you return to your vehicle. When you shop, dress comfortably. Wear shoes that provide you with the maximum balance potential and clothes that allow flexibility for a physical response. Don't handicap your ability to respond.

Walking for Health

When you go for a walk or jog, consider carrying light hand weights. They provide an excellent cardiovascular workout, but they can also be used as a defense tool. If you are assaulted, you can use them as projectiles. They may strike the attacker and cause damage, but mostly they create a moment when the attacker must try

Hand weights provide an excellent workout and can be used as defensive tools.

to avoid being hit, and that gives you an opportunity to run. Also, they are good as projectiles if you are faced with an animal attacks such as a wild dog.

The Internet

The Internet is a versatile information technology with a variety of applications. Just as you must exercise caution in public, it is important to be aware of criminal exploitation of the Internet and to observe the same precautions that you would in public. Be cautious when online interactions become personal in nature.

Realize:

1. Their physical appearance may not actually be how they describe themselves. Even pictures they post online may not be of themselves.

2. They may not live where they claim to live. Even though they may say they live in another city or state, they may actually live close by.

3. Don't give out personal information, such as your home address, phone number, *et cetera*.

Meeting Face-to-Face

Before you agree to meet anyone that you have only communicated with online, take the following precautions:

1. Confirm that the person is who they claim to be. Do you know anyone who knows them personally? Ask them where they work and live. What are their phone numbers? Can you call them at their place of employment?

2. Arrange to meet in a public place on your terms.

3. Bring a friend along. Insist on a meeting at a restaurant or social event with a group of people.

4. Have your own transportation to and from the meeting or date.

Harassment

Always report any conduct that you find obscene, threatening, or offensive to the service provider. Most service providers have instructions for filing a complaint. Print and keep a copy of the offense if possible. Also record any contact information you have such as their email address. Follow the same rules as an obscene phone call.

Use the same precautions when talking to strangers online as you would meeting face-to-face.

Using an ATM (Automatic Teller Machine)

An ATM provides a criminal with an opportunity to plan an assault because it in a predictable location and the target will be carrying money. Following these steps can help reduce your risk.

1. Avoid using an ATM at night. If you must withdraw money after dark, choose an ATM in a well lit area, preferably inside a store or bank lobby.

2. Have your card in your hand before you approach the ATM.

3. Put your money away before you leave the ATM area.

4. Be aware of people around you. Conceal your PIN number as you enter it, and look out for camera phones that can record your PIN number or credit card number.

5. If you use a drive up ATM, make sure all your other windows are up and your doors are locked.

6. Use your bank card as a credit card rather than a debit card because it will minimize how often and the number of places you make your PIN number available.

Be aware of your surroundings and cover your PIN as you enter it.

Section Two:
Verbal Responses

Women's Self-defense in a Nuisance Situation

The object of self-defense is to protect yourself against injury, not to hurt someone else. Low-key techniques are common in the realm of self-defense and can be used to discourage a nuisance situation. The social atmosphere of some situations may make it more likely for a man to put his arm around your shoulder or waist. If you feel this behavior is unacceptable, it is important to make your disapproval obvious before taking physical action. You must immediately end the situation with a serious verbal rejection. Sometimes embarrassment or the social circumstances may influence you to remain silent when speaking up could prevent the situation from escalating before any misunderstanding occurs on the part of the male. If they don't remove their arm, you must take physical action. An early response to the situation, whether verbal or physical, can alter the direction it will take and make a difference in your safety.

When they put their arm around your waist or shoulder, they have made themselves very vulnerable to the effective use of your elbows. You can easily strike to the lower ribs or solar plexus area which will take the wind out of them. If you choose to take physical action, be sure you are justified. The best self-defense skills are awareness and avoidance, but sometimes a situation develops that cannot be foreseen, and action must be taken. When you must take action, do not hold back; use all of your strength. It's more difficult to hurt someone bad enough to allow you to escape than you may think. You want your first physical action to work so that it is last.

1) Verbal rejection.

2) Raise your elbow and reinforce it with your other hand.

3) Strike to lower ribs.

4) Leave the situation.

Before a Physical Response

The Crandall System of self-defense incorporates and teaches physical actions including strikes and kicks as a means to escape physical assaults. Some assault prevention programs recommend you wait it out and look for a chance to run, even if it means being raped and left there. Some proponents of these programs may believe that the Crandall System has chosen violence over logic. On the contrary, the Crandall System has logically chosen both methods of action in their proper perspective and most effective timing. Physical action is a last resort. If it is possible to talk your way out of a situation, please do. There are some things that you can say that may help.

Since the assailant is intent on sexual action, you can indicate that you have syphilis, gonorrhea, herpes, or AIDS. Please, not all three or he will never believe you. There is no way they can check, and the fact that you could be telling the truth may take away the pervert's sense of a romantic moment. Pretending you are going to vomit is very effective. Better yet is to bend over, cover your mouth, and insert a finger into the back of your mouth to stimulate your gag reflex in an attempt to actually vomit. If you can vomit, try to get it on your clothes and body. Repulsion is your goal. It may seem drastic, but don't overlook the option for a bowel movement. Cleaning up at home is faster and easier than healing at a hospital.

Section Three:
Striking Points

Freeing yourself from a grab does not necessarily free you from a dangerous situation. This position may result in you needing to take more definite action. The following diagram indicates seven of the best areas to strike while defending yourself. The most effective striking area is the knee.

The effectiveness of striking these areas will depend on:

1. The technique used.
2. The amount of power projected on point of impact.
3. The type of clothes, including shoes, which are being worn by the attacker.

Effective Targets:

1) Eyes
2) Cervical Vertebrae
3) Clavicle
4) Elbow
5) Solar Plexus
6) Groin
7) Knee

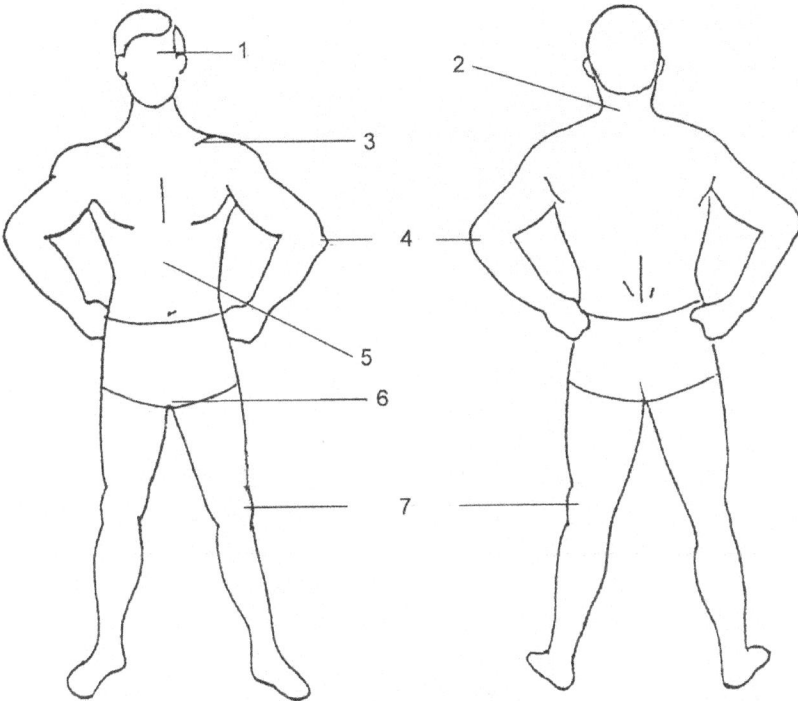

The intent of self-defense is to ensure that you are not harmed rather than focusing effort on hurting your attacker. However, as you defend yourself, the attacker may become injured, but it should only be viewed as a side effect of escaping from a dangerous and possibly life-threatening situation.

Whenever possible, first verbalize your disapproval of actions taken towards you before committing yourself to physical action.

Section Four:
Physical Responses

Defending Yourself in Your Home

The thought of a home intrusion is frightening. Your home is where you should feel safe and able to lower your guard. You may feel more compelled to stand your ground and fight an intruder in your home than on the street because it is your most personal space. However, you should still choose to retreat to a safe room or flee the house instead of a physical confrontation. If this is not possible, you may need to defend yourself physically.

Your home should also be secured to prevent an intrusion. Level four of the Crandall System deals with several ways to improve your home's security, but if there is an intruder, you may need to defend yourself. Many people ask the question, "What should I use to defend myself in my home?" Guns and knives are poor choices as defensive tools. They can be taken and used against you. In addition, a gun can be used in a further crime. A baseball bat is a poor selection, as well. Even in the darkness it can be seen easily, and it's awkward and difficult to wield. Once you swing a baseball bat, its structure and momentum prevent it from being redirected or swung again quickly. The same is true for a fire poker. While a fire poker is shorter, it is often very heavy and hard to direct.

A golf club is an excellent tool for self-defense in the home. It is designed for swinging. When it makes contact with the body, its impact is focused and penetrates through the muscle directly to the bone. If you darken the metal shaft with electrical tape or paint, it will be hard to see in the dark. In addition, the golf club is not a turn around weapon. An assailant wants to put his hands on you and be in direct physical control. If he gets the golf club, he will throw it down because the length of the golf club prevents him from getting close enough to grab you. This gives you and opportunity to pick it up again. The golf club is even useful for times when you are investigating a noise outside your home at night. It can be used to poke the bushes in the dark, yet it is still a weapon available to you outside.

Proper Fist

Knowing how to make a proper fist was covered in Level 1, but because it is important, it will be reviewed here. When you must use a fist to defend yourself, proper form protects your hand from injury during the technique.

First: Begin with your hand open and palm up with the fingers flat and the thumb to the side. Fold (or curl) your fingers down onto themselves and into the palm of your hand.

Second: Now that the fingers are closed and tight, place your thumb over the first two fingers.

> **Note:** Never fold your fingers over your thumb with it in the center of your fist. If you strike with your hand in this structure, you risk breaking or dislocating your thumb upon impact.

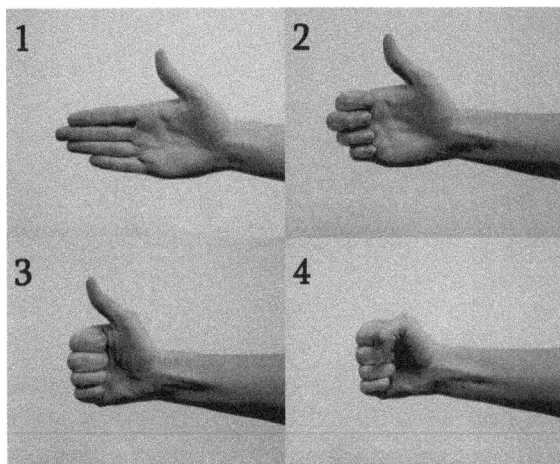

1) **Start with an open hand.**

2) **Fold the first knuckles down.**

3) **Fold the second knuckles down.**

4) **Place the thumb over the first two fingers.**

The hand is now closed into a proper fist. Strike with the first two knuckles of your hand when you punch. The fingers with these knuckles are reinforced by the thumb, and striking with the first two knuckles both protects the joints of your hand and maximizes the effectiveness of the strike. If you have long fingernails, you may have some difficulty forming a proper fist because they will dig into your palms. This discomfort is okay for the short time you will need to maintain a proper fist in a self-defense situation.

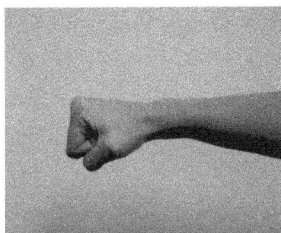

Side View of Proper Fist

Side Kick

There are many different types of kicks in the martial arts, but two are most often recommended for self-defense, the center kick and side kick. The center kick, covered in Level 1, is a very effective kick, and while it is easier to learn than a side kick, it requires a greater degree of accuracy because it penetrates with the ball of the foot. A side-kick strikes with the outside edge of the foot, and this wider surface makes it easier to successfully hit the knee. The force of your strike will be transferred to the knee if you impact anywhere between three inches above or below the joint.

Kick to the attacker's knee.

How to Execute a Side Kick

1. Raise your right knee and blade your foot. To blade your foot, rotate your ankle so that the outside edge of your foot is closest to the floor as if you were walking on the sides of your feet. Pull back your toes and keep the ankle rigid so that the heel of the foot is leading as in Picture 2.

2. Pivot on your left foot so your body turns to face your left side, and bring your right leg around to the front of your body. Your knee is still raised. Keep your eyes on the attacker.

3. Lock your leg down, striking into their knee with the blade of your foot.

4. Recock the leg back up high once done in case you need to kick again. When you are done, place it back on the floor.

You do not need exceptional balance to use this kick. First, the kick does not need to strike any higher than the knee of your attacker. Second, you will be able to grab onto the attacker, a car door, or some other support while you are standing on one leg. This will greatly improve your stability. You can practice this kick at home by using a chair or edge of a table for support.

You can use a chair to assist your balance when you practice kicks.

1) Stand with your feet side-by-side and hold a guard to the front.

2) Raise the knee high and blade the foot, pulling back the toes.

3) Pivot on the foot on the floor so your leg is now to the front.

4) Kick down to the knee, leading with the heel.

After completing the kick, recock the leg as in Picture 3 and return it to the ground as in Picture 1. Practice by repeating these steps.

A Note About Level Three Techniques

In addition to the following level three techniques, you may wish to review the level one escape techniques found on pages 35-39, and the level two techniques found on pages 51-70. Remember, each level of the Crandall System builds on the knowledge of the previous level. While levels one and two are aimed at safety for children and teenagers, the techniques and information presented can also enhance your self-defense skills.

Throat Grab with Counter

A single-hand throat grab is a common assault grab used against children and women. An attacker uses a throat grab to gain control over a person and to impose a state of fear. When grabbed by the throat, a common reaction is to become rigid and unresponsive because the subconscious mind is searching for a response to restore normal breathing. The second most common response is for you to grab the assailant's arm with both of your arms. In this situation, you have tied up both of your weapons, your arms, but you still haven't done anything to free yourself or restore normal breathing. The conscious mind interprets the situation as a helpless one and registers fear. Fear is a complacent state, a state of inaction, and the attacker gains control of the situation.

You can do something. The solution to this dilemma and feeling of helplessness is to arm the mind with the knowledge of how to free yourself in this situation.

Getting Free:

Make a proper fist with the same arm as the person who has grabbed you. For example, if you are grabbed by the attacker's right arm, counter

with your own right arm. Hold your forearm vertical so the fist is directly above your elbow. The fist should be about shoulder height and your arm should be bent. Rotate your upper body and strike the inside of the attacker's forearm near their elbow. As you strike the attacker's arm, turn your head slightly in the same direction as the strike. It is important to strike the forearm on the side of thumb, allowing less grabbing by the attacker as the block drives the attacker's arm from the throat.

1) The throat grab.

2) Make a proper fist, and raise it so that it's shoulder height and above the elbow.

3) Strike into the attacker's forearm, pivoting at the waist.

Adding the Counter:

Once free from the grab, you may still be in danger and need to take further physical action. Use the fist of your right hand, which has just completed the strike to the forearm, to strike the side of the attacker's head at the temple. Do this by bending your right arm, bringing your right fist up to your left shoulder, and pointing your elbow toward the attacker. Turn your fist so the palm side faces your body. Extend your arm out with power and speed to complete the strike. The strike should impact the right side of the attacker's head at the temple, the area on the side of the head between the eye and the ear.

4) Point elbow at attacker.

5) Strike to the temple.

6) Flee to a populated area and seek help.

Double Throat with Open Fingers to Face

If an attacker grabs your throat with both hands, you must react quickly because otherwise you could pass out from a lack of oxygen. Through training, you can avoid your first impulse to grab their arms back. Step forward and turn your body so your left shoulder is leading. Thrust the fingers of your left hand into their face. If you keep your fingers loose, you will not hurt your fingers, but one may strike an eye and cause them to let go so you can run free.

1) The double throat grab.

2) Bring an open hand up to the attacker's face.

3) Drive your open palm and fingers into the face.

4) Push their arm away as you turn.

5) Flee to a populated area.

Defense against double throat grab.

Cross Wrist Grab

1) The Cross Wrist Grab.

The attacker grabs your right wrist with his right hand. Open your right hand and bring it up so the palm is facing you and the hand is directly above the elbow. Continue this motion by bringing your hand down to your right side with the palm facing the attacker. The outside edge of your wrist will now be on top of the attacker's wrist. This quick and small circular motion straightens the attacker's arm, releases their grip, and causes them to draw their shoulders (and head) slightly forward and down toward your open palm. Step forward with your left leg to the attacker's right side. Move forward and past the attacker by stepping with your right

2) Free your arm from the grip with a quick circular motion. The edge of the wrist is on top of their wrist.

3) Step forward and thrust your open palm up into the base of the attacker's chin.

leg to the attacker's right side. On this second step, thrust the palm of your right hand up and forward with power and speed into their base of their chin. As you move past the attacker, push up and forward on the attacker's chin. This will tilt their head to the ceiling and their body will respond by arching their back and shifting their hips forward. This takes their eyes off you so they cannot see you, startles them with a strike to head, and puts them off balance. As you move quickly past them and they begin to fall backwards, keep moving and pushing. This will result in them falling backward onto the ground. You are now free to run.

4) Continue to walk forward and push, tilting their head back.

5) As you move past the attacker, and continue to push they will fall backward.

6) You are free to run to a populated area and seek help.

Bear Hug

1) The Bear Hug.

A bear hug is used to restrain your arms and upper body movement so that you can be pulled into a van or alley. This grab prevents the attacker from punching you because they have committed both hands to the grab. They may have lowered their center of gravity if they need to bend over to grab you. This makes it difficult for them to move freely. With practice, the following technique can free you from this situation.

Step to your right so your feet are side-by-side and a little wider than the width of your shoulders. As you step out, lift your left arm to your side and over your head as if pointing at an angle to the ceiling. Also, extend your right arm out so it points at an angle down toward the floor. Both arms move and the same time and in synch with stepping to the right. The combination of these motions drops your center of gravity and angles your shoulders so that the attacker's arms rise up and off of the core of your body. Their arms still encircle you, but now your arms have enough range of motion to complete the technique. Next, grab the attacker's right arm with both of your hands. Your left hand should be on their forearm, and your right hand should be on their upper arm. Bend straight forward at the waist and pull down on their arm. This will pull the attacker along the core of the center of your back and distribute the weight to the strength of your legs. Continue this motion by rotating your body at the waist to your left and pulling their arm down to your left side. The combination of bending forward and rotating at the waist will result in the attacker falling in front of you on your right side. You will be free to run.

2) Step to the right and angle your shoulders by raising your left arm at an angle.

3) Grab the wrist with your left hand, and grab the upper arm with your right hand.

4) Bend at the waist, pulling down on the arm and bringing the attacker along the center of your back.

5) Rotate your body at the waist, and pull the attacker's arm down to your left side.

6) The attacker falls in front of you on your right side.

Restrained in a Prone Position

1) Being restrained on the ground.

2) Strike with a fist to outside of the attacker's elbow.

3) Palm heel strike to the chin.

If an assault escalates to a position where you are laying on your back and the attacker is straddling your body, there are a couple of ways to get free. Most of them are very complicated and do involve a degree of training. With that in mind, consider the following scenario as an example and see what could be done. In an effort to control you, one of the assailant's arms will be on your chest or throat. In order to restrain you, this arm will lock at the elbow. Strike the outside of that locked elbow with your fist as hard as you can. The trauma to the elbow will cause their head to drop closer to your own. Immediately use your other arm and follow the first strike with an open palm strike that impacts their chin, face, or eyes. Hitting any of these points will drive back their head. Use both of your arms to push their head over to one side. This will shift their body off of you and allow you to roll free to the opposite side. Get up and run for help.

4) Hand pushes head to the ground.

5) Roll free and flee for help.

Choke Hold

The attacker grabs you from behind with their right arm going over your right shoulder and encircling your throat. Turn your upper body slightly to the left, away from the crook of their elbow. Then quickly twist your upper body back to the right. This will create an area of space and movement, which will now allow you to swing your right arm up and behind the attacker. At this point, with your right hand, you should grasp the hair of the attacker or the collar structure of the coat or shirt the attacker is wearing. At the same time, you should now place your right foot out approximately eight to twelve inches to the side and use your right arm to pull the attacker's head down and around in front of you. The attacker will stumble over your sidestepped right foot and fall on his back directly in front of you. At this point, you can flee the area. See page 67 for another view of this technique.

1) The Choke Hold

2) Grab the attacker's arm and collar or hair.

3) Pull the attacker over your hip.

4) The takedown completed.

Knives

For most people, the scariest type of assault involves a knife. Guns can be deadly weapons, but more people can relate to being cut than shot. The fear a knife can generate tends to be greater because the mind can imagine having your face cut, having your body slashed, losing of an eye, receiving stitches, and all of the other medical aspects of a knife injury, and the realization that you will probably live through the attack. Your greatest protection against a knife is to create distance between you and the attacker. Once you are out of the knife's range, it will not be able to harm you. The assailant will tend not throw the knife at you. To do so would be to throw away their weapon, and without the knife, they lack the confidence to assault you. Few knives are properly balanced to be thrown so they will penetrate a target. Add to this the complexity that you will be a moving target as you run away, and it becomes nearly impossible for them to touch you. Therefore, the key element in protection from a knife is distance. Do anything that will create space and a moment when you can flee. Grab a chair and hold it between you and the attacker. In your home you could grab a toaster or a pan from the kitchen counter and throw it at the attacker. You can run away in the moment when they must avoid being hit.

If you are left with no other option, defend yourself. If you succeed in taking the knife from the attacker, under no circumstances allow them an opportunity to take back the knife. When you flee, take the knife with you. If you don't feel that you can hold onto the knife, throw it on top of a building, in a lake, or in a federal postal box where the police can recover it but the attacker cannot. The assault will not continue without the knife.

Information About Knives

Most people picture a knife attack as a long, shiny blade stabbing downward from overhead. While this is a common attack, it is not how an assailant skilled with a knife will assault you. The following points will familiarize you with how a skilled assailant uses a knife. This information will allow you to better assess the severity of the situation as you make your choice to defend yourself.

1. Most knives are designed for cutting, not for stabbing. An individual who places their index finger along the blunt side of a knife is preparing to slash. This hand posture allows them to simply wave their outstretched finger back and forth in front of them, and slice whatever it touches. In almost all instances, a cut is a more severe injury than a stab wound.

2. Some knives have two cutting edges. The tip of the knife that extends beyond the index finger can be sharpened on both sides. This allows it to cut in both directions during a slashing attack.

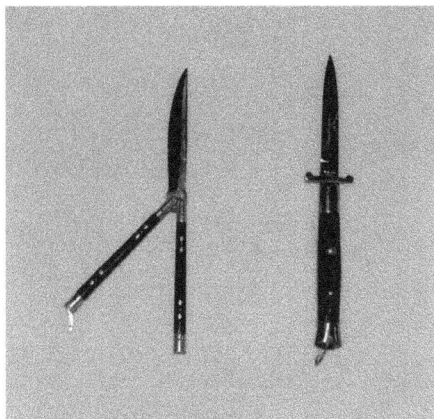

In these situations, it is important for you to immediately recognize that you are not confronted with an amateur, but a skilled criminal.

Examples of knives that are often used as assault weapons.

Training with Knife Techniques

As an author and martial arts instructor, I do not presume that reading these techniques is sufficient to gain the competency necessary to defend yourself against a knife attack. These techniques become effective through practice. A person who is keenly aware of self-defense, trains regularly, and engages in physical exercise will become proficient with time. For an amateur with little, if any, training, defending against a knife is very unlikely. A person skilled in self-defense will find that the following techniques will add to their base of knowledge and further enhance their skills. Most people will never be confronted with a knife assault, but some people have professions that put them into situations where they are more likely to be assaulted with a knife, and they know it. For these people, training with a qualified instructor becomes more essential. Even with proper training, those who understand the quickness of knife moves also understand that you may still be cut.

Overhead Knife Attack

The attacker uses his right arm for the attack. Block into their forearm using a left high block. Keep the hand of your blocking arm closed, and leave your arm in contact with the attacker's forearm. Step forward to their right side with your right leg. As you step, weave your right arm under the attacker's arm, and wrap your right hand over your left closed fist by cupping your hand. Finally, step around with your left leg so you turn your body to face the attacker's side, and apply leverage down on their arm. Doing this final motion quickly will drop the attacker to the ground so you can flee. Exercise caution when practicing with a partner so that you do not stress your partner's shoulder joint.

1) Block the attacker's forearm with a high block.

Close up of interwoven arms.

2) Weave your right arm under the attacker's arm and grasp your left arm's closed fist to take control.

3) Turn to face the attacker and apply pressure to the joint.

4) Take the attacker to the ground so you can flee.

Low Knife Attack

The attacker uses his right arm for the attack. Block the attack by grabbing the attacker's right wrist using a double hand arc grab. This is

done by overlapping the thumbs and cupping each hand. Next, lift the attacker's arm up overhead by swinging it toward your right. This lifts their arm across the front of their body. At the same time, step slightly between you and the attacker by moving your left foot. Pivot your feet so you turn your back to the attacker, and bring the attacker's arm over your head to your right shoulder. Step around with your left foot so you are standing next to the attacker's right side. Facing forward, place their right shoulder against your right

shoulder. The shoulders do not have to be exactly next to each other; there is room for variance. Make sure to bend their arm at the elbow. Finish by pulling down on their arm. This will drop the attacker to the ground so you can flee. Exercise caution when practicing with a partner so you do not stress your partner's shoulder joint.

1) Block the attack by grabbing the attacker's wrist with a double arc hand.

2) Step in and lift the attacker's arm overhead to your right.

3) Pivot and bring the attacker's arm over your head to your right shoulder.

4) Step around with your left leg and bend the arm back.

5) Pull down on the arm to take the attacker to the ground.

Knife Attack from Behind

The attacker stands behind you and places the knife across your throat or against the side of your neck. The attacker is holding the knife in his right hand. Their other hand may be holding your left shoulder.

1) **Knife to the throat from behind.**

Grab the attacker's right wrist by placing the palm of your right hand to the outside of his wrist. This will help control the hand that is holding the knife. Step your left leg behind the attacker's left leg. As you step, slip your left arm between you and the attacker, and place your hand in the middle of their back. It is important to turn toward your left so the knife is off your throat. Slip your head free by ducking under their arm, and step back behind the attacker. You will now be behind the attacker. While escaping from this situation, the knife may become embedded in the attacker.

When you are defending yourself, your intent is never to harm the attacker; however, during the process of protecting yourself, the side effect may be that the knife enters the attacker's body.

2) **Grab the attacker's wrist with your right hand.**

3) **Step back and place your left hand to the middle of the attacker's back.**

4) Slide your head under and keep the knife to the front of the attacker's body.

5) Step back and push your hands together to direct the knife toward the attacker's body.

Back view of above picture #4

Back view of above picture #5

Guns

In some assaults, guns are used as a tool of intimidation. Unlike knives, a gun is effective over longer distances. Therefore, if your intent is to neutralize the gun, you must close the distance without attacking them. Understand that even though their intention may not be to shoot you, they may. If they ask for your possessions, you should comply. It is not worth risking your life over money, jewelry, watches, a purse, or other material objects. However, if they tell you to go somewhere with them, you should take a stand.

Information Regarding Guns

There are a variety of types of guns including long-barreled ones like the rifle and shotgun. In self-defense, we are concerned about pistols. Pistols come in a number of sizes and shapes, but you can become familiar with the guns and how they function. Guns gain their power through ignorance. Whatever your personal feelings toward guns, you should not fear them

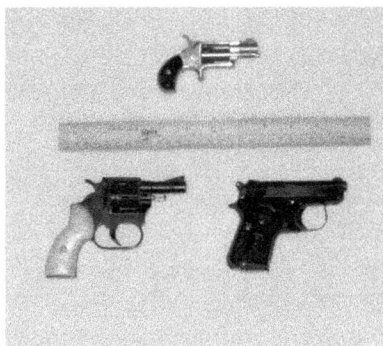

Some examples of handguns.

or be ignorant of them. Contact a local shooting range or enroll in a hunter's safety course. While you may never own a gun, by learning about them you will empower your mind with the confidence to handle one if you must during a self-defense situation. Arming your mind with knowledge is the first step in not becoming a victim.

Training with Gun Techniques

Part of the Crandall System includes defense against a gun, but effectively disarming an aggressor who wields a gun is a complex skill that requires training and confidence. Just as I would not expect you to gain the ability to defend yourself against a knife by only reading these techniques, the same holds true for gun techniques.

Learn more about knife and gun techniques from the resources in the Supporting Materials Section of this book on page 155.

Learn Takedowns Plus Counters Against a Knife and Gun by Grandmaster Clifford C. Crandall, Jr.

Gun to the Front (Upright

The attacker holds the gun in his right hand and aims it at the center of your body. Raise your hands in a motion of compliance until your hands are parallel with the level of the gun. Twist at the waist and grab the gun with your right hand, pushing it to your left side (toward the outside of the attacker's body). If the gun uses a hammer to fire, you may be able to get one of your fingers into that area and prevent the gun from firing. Reach with your other hand and grab the barrel from the top down. Don't allow your hand or fingers to overlap the end of the barrel in case the gun does discharge at this point. You are now in control of the angle of the barrel and movement of the gun. Step back with your right leg and pull with both hands and arms, using the strength of your hips. This will tear the gun free from the attacker's grip. Step back to create distance so they cannot regain control of the gun. When you practice with a partner, be aware of whether or not your fake, practice gun has a trigger guard. Be careful when taking the gun away because it could trap your partner's finger.

If you have gained control of the gun and are in a position to run, do so, and take the gun with you. Contact the police and file a report. If you feel you must discard the gun, safeguard it by dropping it into a federal mailbox or

1) Gun to the front in an upright position.

2) Twist at the waist and grab the gun near the attacker's hand.

pond, or by throwing it on top of a building, away from where a child could pick it up and accidentally be harmed. If the criminal wants the gun, they will have to abandon pursuing you, and they will not find it; however, the police will recover it with a more thorough investigation.

Close up of controlling the direction of the gun's barrel.

3) Grab the barrel of the gun from the top down near your other hand.

4) Step back with your right foot and pull the gun to your hip.

5) Step back to create distance between you and the attacker.

Gun to the Front (Sideways Position)

Some people will hold a gun sideways so the palm of their hand faces the floor. They may do this because they have seen it on TV or in movies, or they may do it to change how the gun moves in response to the recoil from being fired. Whatever the reason, this posture changes the dynamics of gaining control of the gun. With a gun held upright, either hand may redirect the gun to either side of your body, and the technique will be effective. With a sideways position, that is no longer true. If the gun is first directed toward the inside of the attacker's body, the webbing structure between the thumb and fingers of the hand holding the gun will prevent it from being taken away. There are techniques to disarm an assailant in that scenario, but they are complex and involve a higher level of skill and training. However, pushing the gun first to the outside of the attacker's body does allow the gun to be taken away in the same manner as an upright gun. The important factor is to notice which hand is holding the gun. If they hold it in their right hand, first push it to your left. If they hold it in their left hand, first push it to your right.

1) Gun to the front in a sideways orientation.

2) Twist and the waist and grab the gun near the attacker's hand.

Close-up of the hands grabbing the gun just prior to taking it from the attacker.

3) Grab the barrel of the gun near your hand.

4) Step back with your right foot and pull the gun to your hip.

Gun from Behind

The attacker holds the gun to the middle of your back in their right hand. This situation occurs less often than frontal attacks because the assailant wants you to see the gun and be intimidated. If you are faced with this situation, knowing where the gun is can allow you to move with more certainty. You may be able to see it in a window or mirror's reflection. Seeing it out of the corner of your eye or backing up so that it touches you can make a difference. Always ask them not to hurt you, and try to get them to talk. When they must listen to and analyze what you are saying, their mind can no longer focus entirely on what they had planned. This distraction will make successfully defending yourself more likely. Step back into the attacker with your left foot, turning your body and raising your left arm. The gun is now pointing along your back, and if it fires, the bullet will miss your back. Bring your arm down on the outside of the attacker's arm, and trap the gun hand against your back with their wrist under your arm pit. Place your left hand under their elbow and lift up. Executing this move with speed and power will overextend the elbow; therefore, be cautious and exercise control with a practice partner. At this point, counter with either a punch or open fingers driven into the face. Open fingers have the potential to find and rupture an eye. Continue to counter until you can take control of the gun.

1) Gun to the back.

2) Turn and look at the attacker.

Remember, gun techniques require training before they will become practical self-defense. Your primary concern in self-defense is to escape without being harmed, not to harm the attacker, but during the process of defending yourself, this may occur.

3) Bring your left arm over the attacker's arm, and turn so the gun points across you back.

View from the other side. Notice the gun is trapped and no longer pointing at you.

4) Bring your arm under the attacker's elbow and lift up.

5) Counter with strikes to the face until you can neutralize the attack.

Section Five:
After an Assault

Giving a Police Description

If you are assaulted, it is important to report the attack to the police. The police will have a better chance of apprehending the perpetrator if you can provide a physical description. Here are details you should try to notice and remember.

Details regarding their body include:

1) Their sex
2) Weight
3) Height
4) Race
5) Hair color
6) Eye color
7) Age
8) Scars, tattoos, or other marks

Details regarding how they were dressed include:

1) Shirt
2) Pants
3) Shoes
4) Hat
5) Tie
6) Coat

Rape Affects More than Just the Victim

One of the most difficult aspects of a rape is how the family members sometimes react. It can be truly one of the most unfair parts of the assault. Sometimes fathers, mothers, siblings, husbands, or even the woman's own children behave as if they had been violated. As crude as it sounds, they react as if their home or property has been abused by someone else. Many times they struggle with their own emotions and forget who was violated. They feel rage and anger and may even direct it at the victim by saying things like, "Why didn't you do something? Why didn't you fight or run?" They were not there. At best, the situation is difficult to describe, especially to someone who lacks the same level of self-confidence or self-defense skills as you. The situation sometimes worsens with a breakdown in communication between each member of the family and the victim. There is no easy answer for how we should better inform family members. This advice is best left to the experts at the rape crisis centers, hospitals, church counseling groups, *et cetera*.

For the woman who may someday face this dilemma, understand that when you choose to defend yourself, you are fighting for your life as you know it. You are fighting for yourself and your family. The criminal who wishes to harm you will also affect everyone who loves and cares for you. Deciding when and how hard to fight is a moral issue you must confront, but if you choose to fight, fight with everything you have. Believe in your mind and heart that no one has the right to do anything to you that you do not want.

There are many myths surrounding rape. Some of these include that only young women are raped; women who get raped were asking for it because they were dressing to be attractive; most rapes occur by strangers; and, women are raped at night in dark alleys. These statements further ignorance, blame the victim, or limit the awareness of the number of places where a rape could occur. Remember, the best prevention against sexual assaults is to take preventative actions to minimize risk, be aware of your surroundings, verbalize your disapproval of unwanted behaviors before they escalate, and learn how to defend yourself if the need arises.

LEVEL FOUR

Senior Citizen's
Self-Defense & Secure Living

Level four of the Crandall System is intended for adults of all ages, but it also presents information specifically geared for senior citizens. In addition, it covers ways to secure your home against intruders or while you are away for an extended period of time. It is the final level of the system, and its goal is secure living, that sense of being comfortable in your daily life and in control of the world that surrounds you.

Section One:
Awareness and Prevention in Daily Life

As we grow older, our lives change in a variety of ways, and at every stage of life it is important to evaluate how those changes affect our vulnerability and our ability to protect ourselves. As we enter our 70s, 80s, and 90s, we should recognize that our bodies are less flexible and less effective at physically neutralizing an attack than an average 30 or 40 year old. Therefore, it becomes more important to utilize logic and wisdom instead of physical measures to ensure our safety. The most powerful and versatile self-defense resource you possess is your mind, which can provide alternatives to physical self-defense. A keen awareness of how to compensate for vulnerabilities with alertness and precautions can prevent dangerous situations from developing and eliminate the need for physical confrontations. For example, using an ATM at eleven o'clock at night increases the likelihood for an assault. A 40 year old, with a greater capacity for physical self-defense responses, may take the chance. However, a safer alternative would be to avoid this situation by using the bank during the day.

Remember, your most powerful asset for self-defense is your mind. This is a fundamental part of the Crandall System's philosophy, and it is an essential element in self-defense.

Social Security Checks

There are times when you are a more appealing target to criminals such as when you carry a larger sum of money. If you receive a social security check, a criminal can accurately predict when you will have the most money, and you should be alert during these times. If possible, arrange for direct deposit of your funds. This will eliminate the need to carry your check to the bank. If you do carry your social security check, keep it separate, but secure, from your purse or wallet. Good alternatives include an inside pocket of a coat that zips closed or the front pocket of your pants. If a robber confronts you, give them your purse or wallet. When your check is separate, you will know that they are not depriving you of a month's means to live, and this will help ensure that you don't overreact and elevate your risk for injury by getting involved in a physical confrontation. There is nothing in your purse or wallet worth your safety even if you have put your check in it. When you receive your social security check, it is a good time to have a friend or family member visit you, especially if you live alone. The added security of extra people is a deterrent for a potential assailant.

Wearing Rings and Jewelry

If you are in an open, public space, such as a park or bus stop, you can disguise rings with large, precious stones as plain bands by rotating them so the gems are facing into the palm of your hand. This will make you less conspicuous while you sit and wait for an extended period of time. Keep necklaces and chains tucked into your shirt. Also be aware that you do not need to wear all of your best jewelry every time you leave the house. If you are only picking up a few items from the grocery store, you may want to dress more casually.

Set ups for Assault

Many assaults are planned. Criminals often attempt to create a situation where they feel in control. One method that criminals may employ to arrange an assault is by causing a traffic accident on a stretch of road fairly abandoned or far from an exit. The criminal will actually hit your car while you are driving so that you both must pull over to assess the damage. When you get out of your car, they take advantage of the situation to assault you, or detain you while an accomplice hijacks your vehicle. Most accidents are just that, accidents. However, it doesn't hurt to be cautious. If you or your passengers are not injured, wait for the police to arrive. Use a cellular phone if you have one. If you suspect an assault, drive to the next exit or populated stop, even if it means further damage to your vehicle. It is better to need to repair your car than to spend time healing in a hospital.

Identity Theft

Identity theft occurs when your personal information is stolen and used without your knowledge to commit crimes or accumulate debt. Some common examples include account takeover (the thief uses your existing accounts to purchase products), application fraud (the thief opens new credit accounts under your name), and driver license impersonation (the thief acquires tickets and fails to pay them). Identity theft victims face a complex challenge because the fraudulent use of their name often spans multiple jurisdictions. It can take years and thousands of dollars in legal fees to correct. It can even lead to accusation of crimes you haven't committed. Therefore, it's essential to take precautions to protect your personal information. When put into practice, the following advice can help make you safer, but it is not a substitute for legal advice or an exhaustive list. For more information regarding identity theft, contact your local privacy or consumer affairs agency.

10 Tips for Preventing Identity Theft

1. Don't give out personal information over the phone, email, or Internet unless you first initiated contact. Delete and do not reply to emails that solicit personal information.

2. Shred all documents that contain personal information. It is best to use a cross-shredder. These documents include old account statements and credit card offers. An identity thief can use credit card offers to open new accounts in your name. Always take your receipts from a purchase made with a credit card home to be shred. Don't discard them at the store where anyone has access to them.

3. Ask questions whenever your personal information is requested. How will it be used? Will it be shared or sold? How will it be protected? How will application forms be disposed?

4. Safeguard your mail. Your mail often contains detailed personal information; therefore, it is a primary target for identity thieves. Don't leave mail in your mailbox overnight or over weekends. When you travel,

you can have the post office hold your mail until you return. Even safer is to have a P.O. Box or a mailbox with a lock. This style mailbox has a slot where mail is deposited and requires a key to open. Deposit your outgoing mail in a U.S. Federal mailbox or inside at the post office to prevent interception.

5. Safeguard your home computer. Use a password to protect your computer and any files that contain sensitive information. The password should contain several characters including numbers, be difficult to guess, and easy for you to recall. If you write the password down, keep it secured in a lock box. Learn about and use current security software to protect your computer files from hackers while you are connected to the Internet.

6. Safeguard your credit. Review your account statements as soon as you receive them. This includes phone records, cell phone bills, and credit card statements. If a bill doesn't arrive on time, contact the company. It may be that an identity thief has intercepted a statement to disguise illegal use.

Review your credit report regularly. Check for discrepancies such as creditors with whom you haven't spoken and accounts you don't recognize. Federal law permits you to receive one free copy of your credit report from each of the three major credit bureaus annually. This allows you to spread out your requests to each agency so that you can review your credit once every four months.

Cancel credit cards you haven't used in the past six-months. Open credit is a target easily identified by criminals who have stolen credit reports.

7. Safeguard your social security number. Don't carry your social security card with you in your wallet. Instead, keep it secured at home. Don't use your social security number on checks or your driver's license. If a company uses your social security number as an account number or if you live in a state that uses it as your driver's license number, see if you can have those numbers changed. Your social security number can be used to open new accounts, to get credit reports, bank accounts, or credit card accounts, and much more.

8. Keep a photocopy of all your credit cards, debit cards, bank accounts, investments, driver's license, and passport. Include expiration dates and customer service contact phone numbers. Secure this information in a filing cabinet or lock box, preferably one that is fireproof. You will need this information if your cards are lost or stolen.

9. Safeguard your PIN number. Be aware of camera phones when using your credit cards or entering a PIN number. These devices can be used to record your PIN number inconspicuously. Block the keypad from view with your body or palm as you enter your number. Also, limit how often you use your PIN and make it available to others. If you can use your bankcard as a credit card instead of a debit card, it will eliminate the risk of entering the PIN number in public and having it stored in a company's computer.

10. Safeguard your wallet by carrying it in your front pocket or an inside pocket of a coat to make it harder for a pickpocket to steal.

If You Are a Victim of Identity Theft

Limit the damage done by an identity thief by taking the following actions.

1. Report the theft to all three credit bureaus.
2. Report the crime to the police. Ask for a report to be issued and get a copy.
3. Call your creditors and speak with their fraud department.
4. Close your accounts and get new ones with new numbers.
5. Contact the department of motor vehicles to report a lost or stolen driver's license.

Helping Others with Directions

This topic was covered in Level 3, but it also pertains to men and women of all ages, so it will be reviewed here. When the driver or passenger of a car asks for directions, the key factor for your safety is to maintain your distance from the vehicle. Ordinarily, people will drop their guard when they believe they are in control of a situation because the other person appears to be dependent on them for help. Helping others is important but should be done with simple safeguards.

Speak loudly to avoid moving closer to the car. Long complicated directions are seldom remembered or used. Give the driver short directions that will involve two or three turns, and then advise them to ask again if necessary. By doing this you will help the person without leaving yourself vulnerable to someone who may have had intentions of harming you.

The greatest tool you have for safety is your mind. Think situations out before becoming too committed. Most people who seek directions are being genuine, but not everyone that asks for help truly needs it. When you help others, use personal safeguards.

Fitness Programs

Part of a secure life is maintaining or improving health. With the growing number of fitness centers opening up across the country, better fitness is now more accessible than ever. Many of these fitness centers offer a variety of classes and workout programs that involve the use of a combination of machines and free weights. If you are new to this, it is worth going with a friend for the first couple of times. This will make you feel more comfortable in an unfamiliar environment, and if they are experienced with fitness programs, they may be able to assist you. Most fitness centers will take the time to go through your routine during your first few visits. Confusion and a lack of familiarity can be discouraging and will stop you far before any body limitation will. One of the hardest challenges you must face is finding time to workout. Meet that challenge with a committed state of mind by consciously choosing to make time in your weekly schedule. Your personal health is worth it. Enjoy your workouts and stay healthy. A good state of health also helps to keep the mind clear and focused.

Weight Belts for Health

Many of you who lift free weights as a means of exercising or building and shaping your body into a desired appearance, may be familiar with a weight belt. They come in many colors and styles. The belt uses the oblique and abdominal muscles to help support the lower back as the center portion of the belt presses against your lower spinal column. If you lift, you should be wearing one, but its usefulness is not limited to the gym. It can help support your lower back in doing other tasks such as digging around the house, carrying large stones, or moving heavy boxes. When you are going to be doing a half-day of lifting work around the house, or helping someone to move, you can put on your weight belt for added support. Lifting or digging increases your chance of injury to your lower back more than weight lifting in a gym because your mind is not in tune with the work at hand. Your attention is divided among the many tasks you are trying to complete instead of being focused solely on your lifting form. If you have strained your lower back before, you know that a little added support is worthwhile. Safety precautions to prevent or reduce possible injuries are always better and easier than the steps needed to heal an injury.

Walkers be Alert

Many people take a brisk walk early in the morning before they go to work or in the evening after they get home. There are some points worth thinking about before you leave to take your walk. Avoid walking through or next to parking lots and unlit streets if possible. Vary your routes, and don't always leave your house and go in the same direction. Making yourself predictable can make you a target along your favorite route. It also makes determining how long you will be away from your home easily predictable. This allows a criminal at the farthest point of your route to contact an accomplice waiting at your home. They will know how much time they have to burglarize your home before you can get back. Avoid predictability by varying your route each time you walk, run, or bike.

A Note for New Runners

Every year when warmer weather arrives, many people consider becoming joggers. Whether your goal is to stay in shape or simply get outdoors, you need to wear good running shoes. You may want to start running right away, and you may be unsure as to whether or not you will stay with it, which makes it is tempting to do your first few runs in your basketball or tennis sneakers. However, running in the wrong sneakers may cause injury to your feet, ankles, calves, or knees, and you may not ever want to run again. The sneakers you wear make a significant difference in your comfort and health. Look for added heal cushion and arch support when choosing a pair of running shoes. This is the only real equipment you will need for this sport; therefore, make it quality equipment. May your jogging experience be both productive and fun.

Jogging and Self-Defense

Nice weather inspires many to begin jogging again. If you are a jogger, you may want to carry light hand weights when you exercise. Hand weights come in many shapes and sizes, and they have many benefits for your overall physical fitness. They work your upper torso and increase the demand on your cardiovascular system. The hand weights are also an excellent tool for self-defense as projectiles against an attack from a human or animal. An attacker must avoid getting hit by them, giving you time to gain the edge in running for a populated area or home for safety. If they do strike the attacker, they can cause pain and sometimes injury which will halt the attack. The skill to use the resources available around you successfully is at the core of effective self-defense.

Keep Listening

Again, when the weather is good, many people get outside by jogging or walking regularly for health. Many people enjoy listening to music and often wear earphones while they exercise. Plugging both ears leaves you very vulnerable, since hearing helps make your mind and body alert to what is going on around you. Losing this sense prevents you from hearing potentially dangerous situations such as children riding bicycles close behind you, the sound of a car driving by, or a dog approaching fast on your heels. But you don't have to stop listening to music to be safe. You simply need to take some additional steps. The type of earphone that inserts directly into the ear makes it very easy to just wear one and tuck the other in your shirt, and allows one ear to listen for dangers. Earphones that are connected by a band over or behind the head can be worn just in front of your ears or with one off an ear.

You should keep music at a low enough volume to still be able to hear your surroundings. This will also help you in with another long-term safety concern. Listening to music too loudly over an extended period of time can damage the tiny hairs in the cochlea, a tiny organ of the inner ear, and cause permanent noise-induced hearing loss.

Another precaution you can take to compensate for decreased hearing is to run with a partner. If your partner is also listening to music, they should follow the same precautions, but simply having another set of eyes to watch for dangers can help reduce your risk. Allow your senses to work for you while you enjoy the outdoors.

For Winter Motorists

Being stranded can make you a target for assault or robbery. For those who live in areas where snow falls, it is a good idea to keep some sand in your trunk. The sand will help wheel-rear-drive vehicles improve stability and traction in very slippery situations by adding weight to the back end. You can also pour the sand onto that slippery section to give you quick, easy traction, which can make a difference in getting your car moving again.

Rinse out a milk jug, detergent bottle, or similar container, fill it with sand, and screw on the cap. You can also keep sand in a cardboard milk container by stapling it closed until you need it. The size of these containers makes them easy to place in the trunk of your car or the back of your van.

If Your Car Breaks Down

If your car breaks down in an unfamiliar city or area of town, remain in your car. If you have a cellular phone, use it to call for help. If you don't see anyone around, get out and tie a white cloth to the radio antenna or side mirror. Once this has been done, get back into the car, lock your doors, and then turn on your flashers. Only keep your windows open slightly, enough to allow a little air circulation while you wait. Don't try to flag another car down for help. If you must exit your vehicle on a busy highway, it is safer to do so from the passenger side.

Prepare your car for a breakdown by assembling an emergency kit that you can keep in your back seat or trunk. You may want to include bottled water (to avoid dehydration in hot summer emergencies), a flashlight, a first aid kit, gloves, a hat, a blanket (for winter emergencies), and a white cloth (for your antenna). You may want to consider carrying a set of jumper cables, but you should only use them in a situation where you feel comfortable with the help. A cellular phone is one of your greatest assets for getting help, but it is also worth investing in a spare cell phone charger for use only in your car. This will help ensure you can reach others. Be sure to keep important documents available including your proof of insurance, registration, and emergency contacts. They may be necessary if you have to speak with a police officer or roadside assistance agency. Also, make a sign with the name of a friend or family member with their phone number, which you will show someone if they arrive and offer to help. Keep this sign in your glove compartment so it will be available. If you feel comfortable with someone who offers their help, remain in your car, ask them to call the number for you, and wait for the help of someone you will recognize. If someone should come and offer help, but you feel uncomfortable with them right away, tell them that help is already on the way and wait for someone else to offer their help. If the individual tries to get into the car, honk the horn, and if the car will still move, start the car and drive away, even if you have a flat tire. The worst you will do is ruin a wheel, and that is truly a small exchange for your health.

Holiday Shopping Precautions

Around the holidays, stores and malls become crowded with people who are shopping for presents, food, or decorations. Assaults and robberies normally increase during this time of year because people who are shopping carry more money on hand than they normally would. Their savings have been withdrawn and Christmas clubs have been emptied for the holiday shopping. They are also carrying more credit cards during this time of the year.

The contents of your wallet or purse are not worth risking permanent injury or your life. Make your wallet or purse less valuable by leaving unnecessary credit cards at home. Divide the money you carry so that if your purse is stolen, you have not lost all of your money. Put some money in a coat or pants pocket. Separate your driver's license from your wallet. This will give you a better handle on your belongings, and, in the long run, you will have more peace of mind.

Securing Holiday Presents

Storing merchandise in your car can increase your vulnerability for a robbery or assault, especially during the holiday shopping season. The visual temptation for someone to break into a car filled with presents is reason enough to be cautious. Even worse is the possibility for an assault. The criminal may wait by the vehicle for your return and attempt to steal the merchandise you carry. The crowded parking situation may also require you to park blocks away from the store or at the far end of the mall's parking lot. These factors can increase your vulnerability. A great deal of your safety simply depends on being alert to what is going on around you.

During the Christmas season, clean out the trunk of your car. Secure items like brightly wrapped presents in the trunk, not the back seat. If you don't have a trunk, carry a blanket or cloth than can be thrown over them in the back seat, making them less conspicuous. Taking steps to deter crime and violence can help you have a safe and happy season.

Car Keys Should Be Ready

Before you leave a store and head back to your car, take your car keys from your pocket or purse and have them in your hand. Don't wait until you are standing next to your vehicle to fumble through your purse or check your pockets. When you have to set your bags down to search for your keys, you increase your vulnerability. This is especially true in the evening. Individuals who are willing to steal are often bold, and being less aware of your surroundings while you look for your keys is a welcome invitation for someone to push you aside, grab whatever you have bought, or assault you. Have your keys ready so you can stay alert even as you enter your car. The best security measures are forethought and preparation.

Babysitters and the Phone

Individuals who care for other people's children, most often referred to as babysitters, have multiple responsibilities. One area of concern is how you answer the phone.

When you answer the phone, do not state that you are the babysitter. Instead, say that you are a friend of the family who is taking care of their child. Be alert that the caller may not be who they claim to be, and they may be a potential intruder. You want them to believe you are more familiar with the house and its layout than they are. "A friend of the family" indicates that you have been to the house many times and will be able to move around the entire house with ease. You may even know the neighbors quite well. This tells an intruder that you would not be on equal ground. They would be strangers in an area with which you were very familiar.

You can also tell the caller that the parents check in regularly and ask to pass along a message. The suggestion that you are in constant contact with others makes you a less appealing target. If they ask when the parents are returning, it is best to say that you expect them home early. Don't give a specific time. This lets a potential intruder know that more people could arrive at any moment; therefore, an assault would be very risky. Remember, what you say over the phone can make a great difference in your safety.

A Spare Key for the Car

Never leave your keys in the ignition or anywhere else in your car for any length of time. You might only be stopping into the store for a gallon of milk or a loaf of bread, but it only takes a moment for a car to be stolen. An amateur thief or a teenager who only wants a joy ride can check the most common and convenient locations where people hide their keys in just a few seconds. For example: under the front driver's mat, the passenger's mat, over the visors, under a front seat, or in the ashtray. Don't make it any easier for an unskilled teenager to steal your car. The professionals can get in and hotwire it in a moment, but your precautions can stop many of the amateurs and kids.

Where can you keep your spare key? You can have an emergency spare key made out of plastic. They are temporary at best and relatively inexpensive, but the convenience is great. They won't rust or corrode, and you can place one in the middle of a piece of wide adhesive tape and actually tape it to many areas of the car. For example: anywhere along the inside curved part of your bumper, or wheels. This key is always there for you in case you lock yourself out of your car, and it becomes a true challenge for a thief to find.

Unfortunately, you will not be able to use a plastic replica if your original key has a computer chip in it. In this situation you will need to have a copy made that contains the computer chip. Place the key in a container that can be stored somewhere in your car that cannot be reached from the driver's seat. A thief will most often sit in the driver's seat and look at the possible hiding places from this perspective. A good place to hide the key is under the cushions of the back seat. It is inconvenient for you to access, but it is nearly impossible for a potential thief to find. This key will now be available if you find yourself locked out of your car in an emergency. You will have the option of breaking a window and using the key to drive to safety.

Door-to-Door Scams

While telephone and Internet scams have become more prevalent, door-to-door scams are still a very real concern, and they are potentially more dangerous because of the risk of a physical assault. Therefore, you must exercise caution when interacting with door-to-door solicitors. Whether they are selling a product, asking for donations or sponsorship, offering to perform home repairs, or making any other request, never invite them into your home to discuss their offer. When you allow them into your home, you allow them to look around and observe the layout of your house. Instead, you should ask them for a phone number where you can contact them and arrange to meet at an office or public place. You may even want to go with a close friend or family member. If they indicate that they are only in the area for the day and their offices are out of town, you should be wary.

If there are special circumstances and you do meet with them in your home, meet in an area where they cannot easily see other parts of the house. Sitting on an enclosed porch or in a front den with the other doors closed will limit the visual information that might later assist them in a burglary or assault. Again, you could ask a family member, trusted neighbor, or friend to visit.

Before you allow a door-to-door solicitor to work on your home, check to see if they are licensed and insured. Appreciate the legal risk you could incur if they are injured on your property. The concept of self-defense extends beyond just the physical. It also includes safeguarding your mental, emotional, financial, and legal life.

If you are satisfied with their offer to work on your house, you should consider one additional risk. While you may feel comfortable with them, remember, they may employ temporary workers from out of town. These employees could also note the layout of your home, burglarize, or assault you.

Whenever you meet with others for the first time, especially those who initiate contact, it is safer to do so on your terms.

Emergency Contact

There are a wide variety of situations where you may need to get help quickly. These could include a medical emergency, a physical injury, or an intruder. In these situations you need someone you can rely on for help because the police may be preoccupied with another incident, or you may be unable to give pertinent information when medical help arrives such as in a heart attack, stroke, or injury with blood loss. You should have the phone number of someone who lives near you who can come over right away. This person should be someone you think of as family even though they may not be related to you. Many times our own family members live too far away to be of immediate help and you need someone who can respond quickly. Their number should be easy for you to dial or stored in speed dial. Also, make sure you touch base with them once or twice each year to make sure it's okay with them to call them in an emergency.

Home Security Devices

Living alone increases your risk for a burglary or assault, regardless of your age. You can give yourself additional alertness by installing some relatively inexpensive devices around your home. Motion detectors placed in your driveway or at a backdoor can illuminate those areas at night. This sudden change in lighting may deter a prowler, but it will also give you some peace of mind knowing that you have advanced warning.

If your hearing has worsened, you may consider some sound alarms at the entrances to your home. They will be louder than the sound of just the door opening. If your hearing is very poor, you can compensate by installing motion detectors for the deaf that will turn on a light when someone enters your home. This visual signal will be easier to recognize than a faint sound.

The full use of our senses is important for successful self-defense, and any items that enhance our senses only add to our security.

An Alarm for Intruders

A home intrusion is one of the most unsettling violations of your safety because your home is your most personal space, and its the place where you relax your guard the most. By securing your doors and windows, arranging your furniture defensively, and taking other precautions, you make it easier to detect an intruder. However, if you suspect someone has entered your home, what can you do? You want to avoid a physical confrontation if possible. You want to draw attention to the intruder without drawing their attention to your location in the house. The intruder wants anonymity; therefore, they will likely leave your home if discovered. However, if their intent is an assault, simply yelling or making noise from your room will only reveal where you are. They may then seek you out to silence you even if they hadn't originally intended an assault. Furthermore, you don't know if they are alone or armed with a gun or knife.

If your car keys come with an electronic keypad that includes an alarm button, you can keep them by your bed at night. You will be able to activate your alarm if you suspect an intruder. It will draw attention to them without telling them where you are.

Arrange Furniture for Convenience

Maneuverability within your own home is essential for daily safety or emergency situations. The aesthetics of a room may be desirable, but defense and safety is a higher priority. If you need to flee from your home due to a fire or intruder, you want clear pathways. Don't arrange your furniture so that it is difficult to get through.

However, if you feel unsafe because of recent neighborhood robberies or you are going to be alone in your home for a weekend, then rearranging your furniture can be used as a safety precaution. This is discussed later in the chapter.

Recognize Home Defense Resources

Part of effective self-defense is recognizing the potential for everyday items to be used as defense resources. Capitalizing on your surroundings can give you the opportunity to escape. Many people think about using mace, a compression horn, pepper spray, or a whistle for protection, but within your home you may not have these items on hand. However, you may be able to get to a can of hair spray, spray cooking oil, a hot pan of food, or a boiling pot of water. All of these items could be used against an attacker. Picking up a chair to interpose between you and a knife attack or throwing a toaster or other small object at their knees, can give you the space and time to get away. Begin to think about what items could help you in defending against an assault in all areas of your life, and you will learn to use what is available in an emergency.

When the Power is Out

During a storm you may lose power, which can put you in a more vulnerable condition. Unless you have a generator, you will be without lights, unable to use a stove to prepare hot food, and without heat in the winter. There are some preparations you can make for these situations. Have flashlights and backup batteries ready and accessible. Keep one by your bed in case you need it in the middle of the night. Be sure that you have food in the house that does not require to be cooked. The type of instant meal that you put into the microwave or oven and heat up is very convenient, but you should have other food if you lack power to cook. Also, it is a good idea to keep some bottled water in reserve. If you are comfortable using a kerosene heater, it can be good as a backup source of heat. As with anything that uses a fuel, there is a risk of fire, so keep flammable objects away from its proximity. Don't overlook the type of phone you are using either. Even if you don't ordinarily use one, keep a traditional phone in your home that can be plugged directly into the wall. The wireless phones are nice because they allow you to move freely through your house, but they draw power from a device plugged into the wall. These phones don't work when they lack power. However, a phone line that plugs directly into the wall draws its power from the phone line itself and will still work in a power outage. This will enable you to call for help if you have a fire, an intruder taking advantage of the blackout, or need assistance for some other emergency.

Cell Phone for the Glove Compartment

By Law, even if you don't subscribe to a phone service, 9-1-1 can still be dialed and reached. This is true even for cell phones. Therefore, if you don't pay for a cell phone service, you can still keep a cell phone in the glove compartment of your car for emergencies. In an accident, you can use it to call for help. Remember to keep it charged, and check its power level periodically. Also, you could keep a cell phone charger in the car and simply keep it plugged in while you drive. Just don't leave it visible when you are not in your car or someone may break in to steal it.

Section Two:
Awareness and Prevention When Traveling

Securing Your Valuables in a Hotel

When traveling, you should take precautions to protect the valuables in your hotel room. No one wants the nightmare of returning from a day of sightseeing to find their room has been ransacked and their valuables have been stolen. A hotel room is not totally secure because the manager has a master key and others employees of the hotel have access. Most hotels now use an electronic key card, but some hotels still use traditional metal keys. In these instances former guests or employees may have made duplicates or simply kept keys of the room you are in. Therefore, it makes good sense to take some precautions.

Although it may be inconvenient, do not leave your valuables in the room. Hotels usually have a safe in which guests may store their valuables, either in the room or at the front desk. Bring a small, nondescript bag to hold extra money, jewelry, passports, or other important items. If the hotel doesn't have a safe, you can ask the manager to keep it in their office. The same small bag can be put in the trunk of your car or your rental car each time you leave, as well. It may seem inconvenient at times, but it makes for a much safer trip.

Things to Consider Before Traveling

When traveling and sightseeing, there are many things to consider. It's a good idea to carry a small book or a sheet of paper containing important information that will be available throughout your travels. Include information such as your insurance company and policy number, the name and telephone number of someone to contact in an emergency, and list of credit card numbers and telephone numbers to call in case they are lost or stolen. You don't want to wait until you get home to call the company if there is a problem.

Note any important medical history regarding treatment of either yourself or another family member. List any allergies that you or your family may have, including to certain medicines.

Many people realize the importance of these preparations but few take the time to do it. If you haven't already done so, let this be the reminder that results in you taking these precautions.

A Free Hand When Traveling

There are so many things to do and see when traveling that at times it seems like we need three or four hands just to carry everything and take pictures. Using a backpack will allow you to keep both of your hands available. The backpack can be used to hold extra clothes, jackets, a camera, food, film, papers, tickets, a towel, *et cetera*. You can take it off and carry it in close situations or when you are seated. It is easy and convenient at an airport and fits easily under the airplane seat. One of the best advantages of using a backpack is that you don't have to set a bag down to pick up your son or daughter. You will be able to hold their hand as you cross busy roads or parking lots at amusement parks. It is good to have both of your hands left free to deal with what is happening, especially if you need to react with a physical response.

A backpack keeps your hands free.

Driving and Sightseeing

During different times of the year, some of us use our cars to enjoy seeing the beautiful sights across our country. One of the greatest freedoms in our country is our mobility. No matter what the driver's age, it's important to remember that sightseeing is done by passengers. Regardless of how beautiful the field, streams, leaves, or wildlife, the driver should move along at a normal speed. If you are the driver and want to see the sights, too, then you should pull the car off the road. Don't simply slow down. Without realizing it, many of us get caught up in the scenic beauty and find ourselves driving 20 or 30 miles per hour in a 55 mile per hour zone. Whether it is a speeder going too fast or a sightseer going too slow, extremes of any kind change the balance of safety and can be dangerous. Let's appreciate our ability to be mobile through safe driving practices.

Baggage and Airports

Many of the new regulations at airports and bus terminals require you keep your baggage with you at all times. Many of the security agents are now simply confiscating the briefcases and luggage that are left unattended. The concern over bombs and illegal trafficking has increased security action in these areas, but it has not eliminated con-artists and pickpockets. If somebody bumps into you or seems to be unusually friendly, be cautious. Insist that they respect your personal space, and don't allow them to get to close. There are people with very quick hands, and bumping into you is a distracting technique for criminals skilled at stealing. It may not be an accident. If it is an accident, your awareness is not going to offend anybody. Your awareness may be the difference between you losing your wallet, purse, or suitcase. May your travels be safe and enjoyable.

Section Three:
Physical Responses

Self-Defense from a Seated Position

A confrontation while you are seated can be intimidating. The aggressor may appear to tower over you, and they may be yelling or threatening you. Most people's natural reaction is to stand up, but a seated position is not as vulnerable as it appears, and standing may not be the best defensive course of action. In order to stand, you must shift your center of gravity by leaning forward. This motion may cause the aggressor to react by striking you, and you are not in a maneuverable position because your body has committed itself to rising. In fact, you may actually add force to their attack by rising up into it.

Realize that while you are seated, you are in a defensive position. For the attacker to grab or strike you, they must lean down to reach you because you are lower. In addition, you have all four of your limbs available to aid you in a physical response. When you are standing, your legs provide stability; however, when you are seated, the legs of the chair or bench provide you with stability.

To neutralize an attack, kick the knee of the attacker's closest leg. You will be able to reach their knee because they must step in very close to be in range to reach you. This strike will prevent the attack from reaching you because their knee will lock and shift their hips backwards, pulling back their attack. This strike alone may be enough to end the assault.

1) The attacker steps close to throw a punch, and you raise your hands defensively.

ABOVE: A strike the attacker's other knee. Striking to either knee will be effective in neutralizing the assault. BELOW: Close-up of the impact to the knee joint.

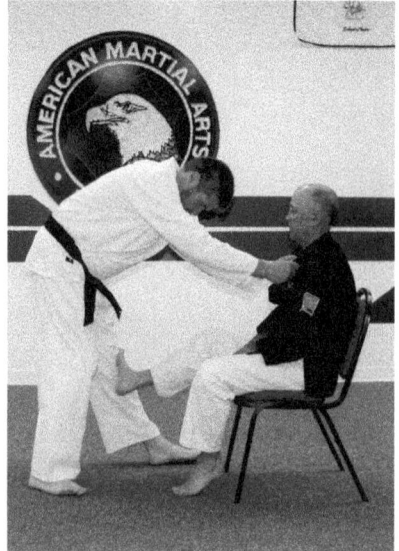

2) Strike to the knee of the attacker to stop the forward motion of the attack. This alone may stop the attack, but you are now also free to counter again if necessary.

Double Throat Grab

1) The attacker grabs you by the throat with both hands.

If someone grabs you with both hands around the throat, they have actually left themselves very vulnerable. As an older citizen, who may have more physical limitations, this technique becomes more essential as a means to escape to safety. Grab both of the attacker's arms to support yourself while you are standing on one leg. Kicking the attacker's knee with either a center or side kick will be very effective. See page 38 for center kick, page 88 for side kick, and page 155 for supporting materials on how to execute kicks. The double throat grab is used in this example, but this technique can apply to a variety of grabs including double-lapel, single-lapel, single-throat, or hair grab. Realize that a kick that impacts from three inches above or below the knee will effect the knee itself.

2) Grab the attacker's arms for support and balance. This will also be a natural reflex to help restore normal breathing.

3) Kick to the knee and lock your leg. Striking anywhere between three inches above or below the knee will be effective.

Double Throat Grab

An alternative way to strike the knee is to rotate the foot so the toes point to the side. This requires more flexibility and practice; however, it increases the area of your foot that can impact the knee and is very effective.

The Walking Cane and Personal Safety

The walking cane is a versatile tool that can enhance your personal safety. It's most commonly used by people with an injury or other physical condition that requires additional support for stability. If you need a cane, you shouldn't be self-conscious or consider it a sign of weakness. Instead, recognize it for what it truly is, a resource for self-defense and an aid for maintaining a healthy lifestyle. Just as glasses or contact lenses assist vision and hearing aids assist hearing, a cane assists mobility. In addition, the cane can be used to neutralize a physical assault.

Use of a cane is not limited to those with stability needs. Anyone can carry a cane. When you go for a walk, especially at dusk or dawn, it provides the added security of carrying a defensive resource. If you are confronted by an assailant, the cane is long enough to prevent them from getting close enough to put their hands on you, and it is even effective for defending yourself against an animal attack. The cane is also inconspicuous. Carrying a stick or walking staff may draw attention, but no one will question why you carry a cane. Even if you don't rely on a cane, it will be available if you accidentally twist an ankle while walking. Learning the following techniques will make you more comfortable with some of the options available to you in a self-defense situation.

It is important to remember that the cane is a defensive resource, but it should not become your sole means of defense. Be vigilant in your awareness. Also, do not forget that you can still use the other parts of your body; therefore, some of the following techniques also incorporate the use of your arms and legs in combination with the cane.

Parts of the Cane

Before learning about specific techniques, you should first become familiar with some terminology that pertains to the cane. Canes come in a variety of styles and sizes. As a defensive tool, the most effective canes possess a curved crook. The main parts of the cane are the horn, crook, shaft, and tip. The horn is the end of the curved handle and can be used for applying pressure to the body. The crook is the curved handle and can be used as a hand-hold to swing the cane defensively or to hook parts of the body. The shaft is the length of the cane and provides a long surface for blocking, applying leverage, or striking. The tip is the end of the shaft and generally is covered with a rubber tip for traction. The tip is useful for thrusts.

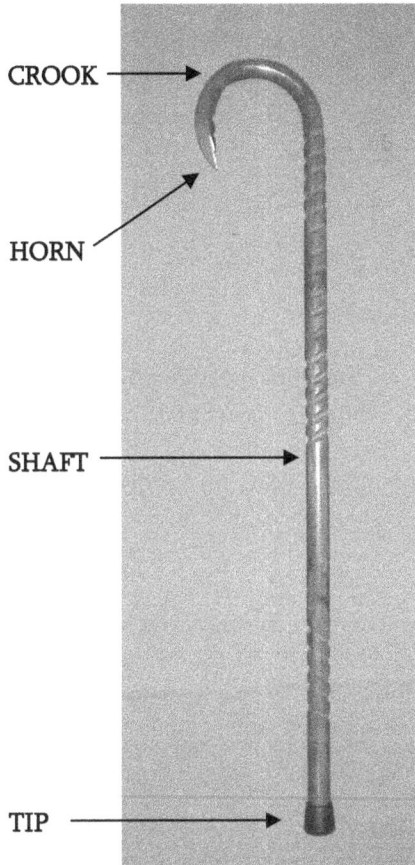

CROOK

HORN

SHAFT

TIP

Creating Space with the Cane

As with any confrontation, you should first verbalize your desire to be left alone. This is especially true when defending yourself with a cane. An onlooker may only see you use the cane and not realize that it was you who was attacked. From their perspective, you could appear to be the aggressor and not the victim. In addition, it should never be your intention to harm the other person, only to protect yourself. Therefore, if you are faced with an aggressor, first yell at them to leave you alone. Back up and hold your hands up, including the cane. Draw as much attention as you can and create space between you and the assailant.

Now if they do proceed with an assault, you are out of their reach, but the combined length of your arm and cane can reach them. Holding the top of the crook loosely will allow you to swing it in front of your body. Practice swinging the cane from left to right and from right to left so that you become comfortable with the motion. Be sure to start slowly and be aware that as the cane approaches the opposite side of your body, you will need to tighten the muscles of your hand to slow and stop the cane to prevent it from hitting you. Swinging the cane is an excellent way to maintain a protective distance between you and an attacker.

Cane Techniques

Bear Hug

If someone grabs you from behind and traps both of your arms against your body, you may feel helpless. This is especially true if one or both of your legs require the support of a cane for movement. When applying a bear hug, the attacker has committed their arms to controlling you and left themselves vulnerable to the effective use of your cane. You will have a limited range of motion for your arms, but even if they grab you below the elbows, you will have enough to escape.

Turn the crook of your cane so the horn points toward your body and grip the shaft just below the crook with both hands. Hook the crook over the attacker's wrists where they come together in front of your body. Pull down sharply. This will release their grip and create a small opening. Step forward with your left foot and turn slightly toward your right side, looking back. Slide your right hand about a third of the way down the shaft. Thrust the tip of the cane back into the center of their body, driving the attacker back. From here you are free to escape or take further action if necessary.

The Bear Hug

1) Position the crook over the attacker's hands.

2) Pull down to break the attacker's grip.

3) Step, turn, grip the shaft, and thrust the tip into the attacker.

4) The attacker is driven backwards and you are free to escape.

Double Lapel Grab

1) The Double Lapel Grab

The attacker grabs the front of your shirt or coat with both hands and curls the material into their fists. You are holding the cane in your right hand. Raise the cane up and bring it down between you and the attacker so that the shaft lies across the attacker's forearms. Grab the other end of the shaft with your left hand on the outside of their arms. Pull down and toward you with both hands, applying pressure to the attacker's arms with the shaft. This will cause the attacker's arms to bend at the elbows so they are drawn toward you, and it will also draw their shoulders down so their head is level with your cane. From here, thrust the shaft of the cane straight forward with both hands to push the attacker away.

2) Bring the shaft of the cane over the attacker's arms and pull downward.

3) Thrust the shaft of the cane forward and push the attacker away.

Defense Against a Punch
(Strike to the Knee)

The attacker steps and punches with their right arm. You are holding the cane in your right hand. Block the punch with the shaft of the cane. To do this, grip the shaft just below the crook and bring the cane up in a circular motion in front of your body, making contact with the outside of the attacker's

1) **Preparing for the punch.**

2) **Step and block the punch with the shaft of the cane.**

forearm. As you block, step slightly forward and to the left with your left foot. This step will help to put you out of the direct path of the punch and avoid being struck. You are now on the attacker's right side, away from their other arm and a potential second punch. Follow the block with a strike to the attacker's right knee with the shaft. To do this, move past the

attacker by stepping with your right leg and bringing the cane down on your right side. The strike to the knee will prevent the attacker from pursuing you. You are now behind the attacker and can either flee to safety or turn to evaluate whether further action is required to defend yourself.

3) **Step and strike the attacker's knee.**

Defense Against a Punch (Takedown)

The attacker steps and punches with their right arm. Block their punch with your left arm using a knife hand block (for more specific information regarding blocking, see the supporting materials section of this book on page 155). Once you have blocked, use the open palm of your left hand to grab the attacker's arm. As you block, bring the shaft of your cane up between the attacker's legs. During this rising motion you may strike the attacker's groin, but that is not your intention. Instead, you want the cane to be positioned somewhere between the hip and knee and parallel with the ground. Now step past the attacker's right side and rotate your right arm so the palm of your hand is facing up and your wrist is straight. This will rotate the cane so that the edge of the shaft near your hand is pushing into the

1) Step forward, block the punch with your free hand, and position the cane between the attacker's legs.

muscles of the attacker's leg above the knee, locking that leg. The other end of the shaft will pivot around to press against the back of the opposite leg's hamstring. By walking past the attacker and pushing forward on the cane in this position, you will use leverage to force the attacker to fall to the ground. From here, you are free to escape or take further action if necessary. Be careful when practicing with a partner. It does not take much pressure on the leg to transfer that stress to the knee joint.

2) Step forward and push on the cane.

3) Your forward movement combined with the leverage of the cane applied to the legs will take the attacker down.

Knife Attack

Defending yourself against a knife is a complex skill with inherent risk. Important information regarding knives was covered in Level 3 on pages 100. For the sake of brevity, it will not be repeated here, but you should review that section before training with knife techniques.

When faced with a knife, your best protection is distance. The length of the cane's shaft added to your arm's length can keep the attacker out of range; however, if you must physically neutralize the attack, there are techniques that can assist you.

Blocking a Knife Attack

A Low Knife Attack

The attacker lunges with a forward stabbing motion for your torso. Grab the other end of the cane's shaft near the tip and raise it close to your body so it is parallel with the floor. Block down into the attacker's forearm with the middle of the shaft. The force of the impact may cause the attacker to drop the knife. Step to the side of the attacker, and let go of the shaft with the hand near the tip of the cane. Bring the cane down in a strike to the attacker's closest knee.

1) Block down into the attacker's forearm with the shaft of the cane.

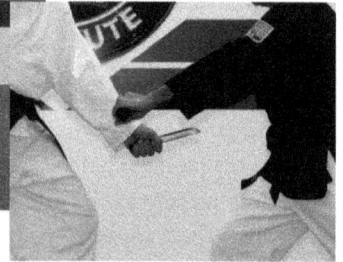

2) Step to the side and strike down to the attacker's knee. Notice that the attacker has dropped the knife as a result of the force of the block.

A High Knife Attack

The attacker stabs downward from overhead. This technique is similar to the low knife attack defense. Grab the other end of the shaft near the tip and raise it close to your body so it is parallel with the floor. Block up into the attacker's forearm with the middle of the shaft. The force of the impact may cause the attacker to drop the knife. Step to the side of the attacker, and let go of the shaft with the hand near the tip of the cane. Bring the cane down in a strike to the attacker's closest knee.

1) Block up into the attacker's forearm with the shaft of the cane.

2) Step to the side and strike down into the attacker's knee.

Sleeve Grab

The attacker grabs your right sleeve with his left hand. You are holding the cane in your right hand just below the crook. Raise the tip of the cane toward the outside the attacker's arm, and place it between you and the attacker so it is across the side of the attacker's neck. The shaft of the cane rests across the back of the attacker's arm near the elbow. Push the cane toward the center of your body, applying leverage across the attacker's neck and on the attacker's arm. This will free you from their grab.

1) The Sleeve Grab.

2) Position the cane across the neck and along the back of the arm.

Close up of the cane's position.

3) Apply pressure on the cane toward the center of your body.

Attacker Grabs Your Cane

The length of your cane allows you to keep an attacker at a distance; however, if the attacker grabs your cane, you may need a way to regain control of your cane without struggling with a lot of strength. Grab the other end of the cane near the attacker's hand (palm down). Step forward and bring the other end of the cane forward up toward the attacker's head. At the same time, bring the other end of the cane back toward your side. Doing this motion quickly will allow you to strike the attacker in the head or collar bone, and either strike will free you to escape.

1) Using the cane's length to create space between you and the attacker.

2) The attacker grabs the cane.

3) Grab the cane near the attacker's hand and step forward, raising the cane.

4) Bring the cane down in a strike to the attacker's head or collar bone.

Double Lapel (Close)

The attacker grabs the front of your shirt or coat with both hands, curls the material into his fists, and pulls you forward. You are holding the cane in your right hand. The first motion for the technique utilizes the length of the cane's shaft. Strike downward to the attacker's instep (the top of the foot). Do this repeatedly until you strike the foot. This strike is effective even if they are wearing shoes. The strike will cause pain that will loosen their grip and distract them. Follow this by raising the cane to the side your body (outside the attacker's arms) and gripping the shaft of the cane near the center. Bring the cane between you and the attacker, and position the cane across the attacker's throat. Step back with your left leg. At the same time, pull on the cane with your left arm and push the other end of the cane forward with your right arm (this is like using an oar). The leverage of this technique will free you from the grab and can be used to take the attacker down to the ground.

1) The attacker grabs the front of your shirt with both hands and pulls you in close.

2) Strike down into the attacker's foot with the tip of the cane.

3) Raise the cane up to the outside of the attacker's body and grip the shaft of the cane near it's center.

4) Bring the cane between you and the attacker and position it across the attacker's throat.

5) Pull back on the cane.

6) Finish by stepping back, and pulling with one end of the cane and pushing with the other.

Defense Against a Punch (Another Takedown)

The attacker steps and punches toward your head with a right punch. You are holding the cane in your right hand. Raise the cane up in front of your body and grab the shaft. Continue this block by raising the tip up so that the shaft of the cane impacts the outside of the attacker's arm. Bring the end of the cane down to the opposite side of the attacker's neck. Pull the cane with your left hand and push forward on the cane with your right hand.

1) Block the punch with the shaft.

2) Bring the cane to the opposite side of the attacker's neck.

3) Pull with your left hand and push with your right hand to apply leverage.

Single Lapel Grab

The attacker grabs the front of your shirt or jacket with a single hand. You are holding the cane in your right hand. This technique uses the same principle as an earlier technique. Grab the attacker's wrist and hold it tight to your body. Bring the cane up between the attacker's legs. Step forward on the attacker's right side, and push forward on the cane. This will apply leverage and result in the attacker falling to the ground.

1) Grab the attacker's hand, and bring the cane up between the attacker's legs.

2) Step forward and apply leverage.

Close up of the cane's position as you apply leverage.

Section Four:
Home Security

Securing Your Home

As you prepare to leave for a vacation or family outing, you should take some steps to safeguard your home in your absence. Have your mail held by the post office or picked up by a trusted neighbor. This keeps it from accumulating and indicating that you are away.

Hook up a couple of 24-hour timers that will turn the lights and radio on and off during your absence. If you hook them up and let them work for a few days before you leave, it will allow you to make sure that they are functioning properly. This will also establish a pattern for a potential prowler. When they see the timers working in conjunction with your presence at home, it makes it more complicated for them to determine whether or not your home is really vacant. Enjoy your vacation knowing that you will be coming back to your home as you left it.

A Safe Room for the Family

We seldom think of retreating to safety in our own home, but it can become necessary. You should have a Secure or Safe Room in your home. This is a room that you can run to in case of an intruder. This room should have a dead bolt or extra lock in addition to the doorknob's lock. A chain style lock is not recommended because it is less secure and allows the door to be opened slightly, giving the intruder some visual information of your location in the room. This room should have a phone in it so you can call for help. If the intruder somehow breaks in, you must be able to get out. Therefore, you need to have another way out of the room, either a window on the first floor or a door that will take you to another part of the house. That door should also have secure locks. A secure room in your home is good step in improving safety for you and your family.

A Doorstop for Security

Most people understand the logic of installing a good lock on the front door such as a deadbolt or combination of two different locks. Unfortunately, an intruder seldom uses the front door. We should be more concerned about the garage door or back door. The back door is normally weaker and has more glass than the front door.

If the door opens onto a tile or wooden floor, a door stop can be used for added security. A doorstop is normally used to hold a door open, but it can just as easily help keep a door closed. The disruption made in opening a door jammed closed with a doorstop will create enough noise to alert you that someone is trying to get in. Just before you go to bed, lock your doors, kick down the doorstop, and sleep soundly knowing your home is more secure.

Knickknacks on the Widow Sill

In the summertime, it is nice to keep the windows open a few inches for air circulation. You can help secure your windows with a very simple type of alarm. Arrange some knickknacks so they sit on the middle of the windowsill, that is, the top portion of the bottom window. These items are unreachable by the intruder, but if the window is raised up, they will fall off and make noise. This is a subtle but effective method to give you advanced warning of a potential intruder.

Arranging Your Furniture Against Intruders

If you have ever walked through a park or the woods in the evening and followed the trails made by the animals, you know that even in the dark of night you can avoid bumping into bushes and trees. With very little light, the paths made by animals or human beings are identifiable. The black and gray shadows of trees, bushes, and rocks can vaguely be identified. This is how your living room appears to an intruder. With no lights on, it is still possible to move through an individual's living room without bumping into chairs, tables, and lamps. This is possible because we create a basic pattern of paths through these obstacles. If you are alone for a weekend, your spouse or roommate has gone away, you may find a little comfort in changing one or two pieces of furniture before going to bed. For example, turn the coffee table so it swings straight out across the living room or move a chair part way into a doorway. A night intruder has an expectation. They have an image in their mind of the normal paths established in a person's living room. They will not normally notice these changes until they have already bumped into the furniture. This disturbance will alert you to the intrusion.

A word of caution: if you are used to getting up in the middle of the night for a drink of water or a general check of the house, be careful because you won't see the change in furniture either.

A Safer Place for the House Key

Most people still leave their house key hidden outside the front of their house; for example, under a rock, in the flowerpot, under the mat, or in a store-bought, artificial rock. If you need a spare key left outside for your own emergency use, place the key to the front door in a place that would be difficult to get at. Preferably, the front door key should be hidden in the back of the house. You can put it in a plastic bag and bury it approximately six inches in a spot near the back door. If someone did find it they would probably spend their time trying to use it to unlock the back door. You can also put the back door key in an area in the front of the house.

Supporting Materials

The Crandall System provides a solid foundation for improving safety and awareness in everyday life for people of all ages, and with that foundation you may wish to enhance your knowledge of self-defense. The following resources are materials that will support your continued learning.

American Eagle Style Textbook

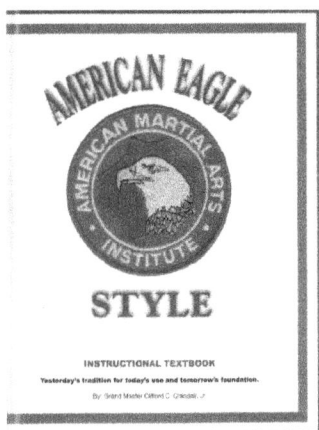

This 324-page, hardcover textbook documents the American Eagle Style of martial arts and includes information on a variety of topics including self-defense, women's self-defense, takedowns, gun and knife self-defense, circular self-defense training, kicks, punches, blocks, and more.

ISBN 0-9636605-3-5

Children's Self-Defense and Awareness, Volume 1 DVD

This instructional DVD presents a self-contained program for use by educators, parents, and community leaders. It covers level one of the Crandall System and includes sections for both children and instructors to view. Some of the material taught in this 60-minute program includes punches, kicks, circuit training, escapes from arm grabs, throat grabs, sleeve grabs, and more.

ISBN 0-9636605-2-7

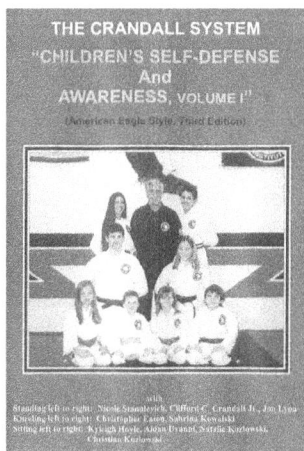

Learn Takedowns Plus Counters Against a Knife and Gun DVD

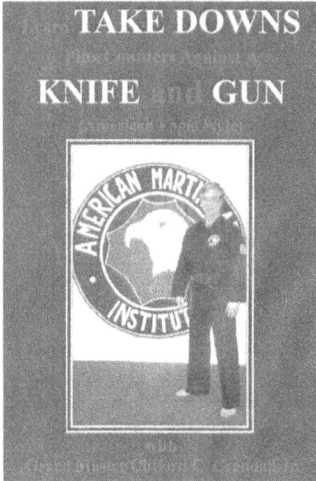

This instructional DVD presents nine takedowns, three from grabs, three from punches, and three from kicks. It presents five counters against knife assaults and five counters against a gun. In addition, it includes proper stretching, tumbling, and the advanced American Eagle Style self-defense techniques, SD-1 and SD-2. The program's length is 59 minutes and 30 seconds.

ISBN 0-9636605-6-X

American Martial Arts Institute Website

This website hosts the official Crandall System webpage that contains information regarding the growth and presentation of the Crandall System. The website also includes the most recent information about the program's designer, this book's author, and contact information. You will also have access to other self-defense and safety related resources.

www.amai-eaglestyle.com

Index